Gayatri Mantra

ओम् भूर्भुवः स्वः तत् सवितुर्वरेण्यम्
भगों देवस्य धीमहि धियो यो नः प्रचोदसात्

Om Bhur Bhuvah Svah Tat Savitur Vareneyam
Bhargo Devasya Dhimahi Dhiyo Yo Nah Prachodayat

Other books by Komilla Sutton:

The Essentials of Vedic Astrology
The Lunar Nodes: Crisis and Redemption

You can visit Komilla's website at

www.komilla.com

Personal Panchanga
and the
Five Sources
of Light

KOMILLA SUTTON

The Wessex Astrologer

Published in 2007 by
The Wessex Astrologer Ltd
4A Woodside Road
Bournemouth
BH5 2AZ
England

www.wessexastrologer.com

ISBN 9781902405261

A catalogue record of this book is available at The British Library

Cover design by Creative Byte, Poole, Dorset.

Printed and bound in the UK by Biddles Ltd, Kings Lynn, Norfolk.

DEDICATION

This book is dedicated to
Dr Ajit Sinha, for showing me the light.

ACKNOWLEDGEMENTS

I'd like to thank the following for their help and support:

Paul F. Newman for his excellent editing and all the hard work he has done to make this book so special.

Margaret Cahill for being the best publisher an author can have, and her inspiration and relentless perfection that makes for such great books.

Swami Sita for her spiritual love and guidance.

Janet Lee for her great friendship.

My brother Kuldip Wirk for always being there for me.

And finally, to my great family who have always supported me, especially Naniji, my uncle M.M Singh and my mom.

CONTENTS

1

WHAT IS PANCHANGA?

Panchanga is the Indian Almanac used from ancient times to tabulate the effect of many diverse cosmic factors that influence the quality of the day, and it is very different from those available in the west. The actual casting of the panchanga requires complicated calculations, as it has to be precise from the place of birth. The Hindu spiritual calendar and its annual festivals are based on it, and it is consulted for the best time for auspicious ceremonies. In most traditional Indian households, the panchanga is consulted daily to know the quality of the day. Panchanga is also used for almost every branch of vedic astrology: natal, muhurta (election), prashna (horary), transits, etc. While many regional panchanga are available annually, it is rare to get one that takes into account a longer period. Fortunately all vedic astrology software calculates the panchanga for any time and place so it should not be a problem to find the panchanga for the day you are searching for.

Panch means five, and Anga means limbs, so Panchanga literally means five limbs – or the five sources of energy that influence any given day. The essence of the panchanga is how the Sun and Moon relate on a daily basis and how these interactions create special awareness for each of us. The condition and the inter-relationship of the five limbs are a conduit through which the power of the luminaries have to pass in order to reach consciousness. If the circumstances created by them are difficult it will be harder to fulfil the potential in the natal chart even if it promises a lot. The panchanga is used to create the awareness and ability to see the promises of the birth chart more clearly.

Panchanga has mainly been used for election in the past, but it is important to understand that it is what sustains the birth chart, and allows us to see it in the right way. This has never been properly understood – we continue to judge the natal chart without looking at the energies that surround the day of birth. Ancient classics like *Jataka Bharnam*, *Hora Ratnam* and *Maan Sagri* have much information on this subject, which somehow was never incorporated into present day Jyotish in analysing natal charts. This book, *Personal Panchanga*, will study how these five forces influence the birth chart.

The Personal Panchanga is the secret key to understanding the deeper levels of your chart, and this book will help decode it. The birth panchanga has far reaching influences: it effects our emotions, temperament and nature. It can give added information about who we are and how we feel. It gives us special consonants which are right for our name, the way we relate to each other, the hidden personality, the right career, the lucky times of life and much more. It can strengthen the effect of the planets and give us additional qualities that we may not understand purely through the natal chart.

The Five Lights of the Day

The panchang is a combination of:

1.   Dina – solar day
2.   Nakshatra – the distance travelled by the Moon in one day
3.   The Tithi – lunar day
4.   Karana – the half lunar day
5.   Nitya Yoga – the daily relationship between the Sun and the Moon

Dina means day. Dina is one solar day that begins at sunrise and ends at sunrise of the next solar day.

Nakshatra means a star in Sanskrit. A star is a point of cosmic light. One nakshatra is how far the moon travels in one day.

Tithi is a lunar day. From their conjunction at the New Moon, the Sun and the Moon move away from each other 12° per day. This 12° of separation is known as the tithi. A lunar month has 30 tithis. Each tithi is slightly shorter than the solar day. A lunar year is 48 weeks.

Karana is half a tithi. Karana is derived from the word *Kar* whose meaning is to do. *Karana* means doing, performing, producing and creating.

Nitya means daily and *yoga* means a yoke or connection. The panchanga yoga is different from the yogas formed by the planets. The yoga is the daily angle that is formed between the Sun and the Moon.

Dina is connected to the Sun and Nakshatra to the Moon; the other three components of the panchanga show the connection between the two luminaries.

Panchanga gives the quality of light with which to interpret the natal charts, and its strength is decided by the condition of the luminaries in the five sources, as just described. If it is strong, then it is easy to understand the message our birth chart is giving. If weak, it creates shadows and we are unable to comprehend what the chart tells us. A strong panchanga illuminates and highlights all we need to deal with life whereas a troubled panchanga makes it impossible to see even the good points of the natal chart. Without the awareness of the panchanga we can be scrabbling in the dark unable to make real sense of our natal charts. Each limb of the panchanga stands alone but how all the limbs interrelate with each other gives the final picture.

The Sun, Moon and the Panchanga

The natal positions of the Sun and Moon are very important. Other planets support the interaction of the luminaries. The quality of the Sun and Moon in a natal chart by rashi, conjunction and aspect will impact on the qualities expressed by the panchanga. If they are weak, despite the panchang promising a lot, it does not deliver to its best level. This is when the negative qualities of the panchanga can take root. Similarly a very negative panchanga can be improved if the luminaries are in dignity and strong in the natal chart. If one is in dignity and the other is weak, it gives more neutral effects. Special emphasis has to be placed on the Moon as the mind can improve and spoil the life the incarnating soul wants to achieve. Many spiritual disciplines are undertaken to strengthen the mind, as a strong and good mind is responsible for making or marring the quality of life. Remedial measures that can be performed for a negative panchanga are detailed in Chapter 8.

The Natal Chart and Panchanga

Consider the relationship between the panchanga and the natal chart in this way: panchanga as the location and the birth chart as a house being built. If the location is wrong, the best or most expensive house there will not be so valuable, whereas if the location is right even a rundown house can be improved and value added to it.

Why Study the Panchanga?

Birth panchanga tells of the burnt signs, the yogi or the good luck points, the lucky and unlucky planets, how to get the right name, the source of your energy, the best career options and relationship compatibility. Panchanga gives so much more information about your personality, its strengths and weakness. After reading this book, you may wonder how you ever analysed the natal chart without using it.

Many authors have written about the panchanga, so this is not new information. What this book provides is a step by step guide to using panchanga on a personal level and it fits the pieces of the jigsaw together.

The Spirituality of the Panchanga

The panchanga is seen as our connection with the divine forces. As the forces of consciousness move from the subtle to the gross level, they start connecting with us through the five great elements known as the pancha maha bhuta. Each of the five elements connect to one of the limbs of the panchanga. The panchanga shows the gross qualities of consciousness as we descend towards materialism but by controlling our inner and outer nature through spiritual endeavours we can turn this quality back from gross to subtle, and the soul can progress to its higher self.

The knowledge of panchanga was considered sacred and prayers were said to it so that it revealed the true spiritual picture to the aspirant. An important part of the incarnating soul is to purify their panchanga through spiritual and dharmic works so that the panchanga quality becomes more subtle, and the light we live in not only highlights our outer world but also brings inner light.

The descent and the ascent of consciousness is given in Chapter 2 along with the story of the five great elements, their relationship to the gross and subtle. Purifying the gross elements and connecting them to the subtle chakras through panchanga shuddhi is detailed in Chapter 9.

How the Chart and the Panchanga Look Together

Here is an example of a vedic chart – showing both the birth chart and the panchanga of the day of birth:

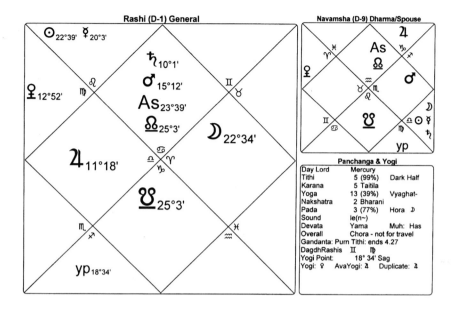

Rashi (D-1) General

Navamsha (D-9) Dharma/Spouse

Panchanga & Yogi

Day Lord	Mercury	
Tithi	5 (99%)	Dark Half
Karana	5 Taitila	
Yoga	13 (39%)	Vyaghat-
Nakshatra	2 Bharani	
Pada	3 (77%)	Hora ☽
Sound	le(n~)	
Devata	Yama	Muh: Has
Overall	Chora - not for travel	
Gandanta: Purn Tithi: ends 4.27		
DagdhRashis Ⅱ ♍		
Yogi Point: 18° 34' Sag		
Yogi: ♀ AvaYogi: ♃ Duplicate: ♃		

Swami Sivananda
Born 8 September 1887
4.16am (IST –5.30 hrs) Pattamadai, India. 77E40, 8N48

Swami Sivananda

Saint, great teacher, yogi, author of many books and founder of the Divine Life Society.

Panchanga for the day of birth:
1. Dina, day of birth – Wednesday, Lord is Mercury
   Hora, hour of birth – Moon
2. Nakshatra of the Moon – Bharani, pada 2
3. Tithi, lunar day – Krishna Panchami, fifth day of the waning moon
4. Karana, half lunar day – Taitila
5. Nitya yoga[1], daily connection between Sun and Moon – Vyaghyat

Additional information from the panchanga:
Sunrise – 06.10
Sunset – 18.26
Akshara, sacred sound – Le

---

1. Nitya yoga is also just given as Yoga in most software. This is different from the planetary yogas in the chart.

Dina nakshatra – Hasta[2]
Dagdha rashi, burnt signs – Gemini and Virgo
Yogi point, auspicious degree – 18°34 Sagittarius
Yogi planet, auspicious planet – Venus
Avayogi planets, inauspicious planet – Jupiter
Duplicate yogi, an added lucky planet – Jupiter

Each one of these aspects needs to be analysed and understood. It reveals amazing details about the personality. Read on to understand how to use this information.

---

2.   Dina nakshatra is given as Muhurta or Muh in most software.

2

THE UNFOLDING OF CONSCIOUSNESS –
FROM SUBTLE TO GROSS

Panchanga shows how the soul is caught up in the play of the illusionary world of maya and pancha maha bhuta, the five great elements. The soul comes down to earth in the form of the living being to mature, develop spiritually and find moksha, but soon becomes involved in the material world. In doing so it loses touch with its higher entity. The darkness of the incarnated world obscures the pure light of the eternal world.

The five great elements are responsible for our desires as they control the senses – so the extent to which the soul is sidetracked into this sensual world is indicated by the condition of the panchanga and the natal planets. To truly understand how the panchanga works we must understand the play of purusha and prakriti and the relationship between the panchanga and the five great elements.

In *The Essentials of Vedic Astrology*, I spoke about the Creation being the product of a meeting between *purusha* and *prakriti* – the male and the female – the soul and the forces of regeneration. Purusha and prakriti is the perfect balance of the three gunas and the pancha maha bhuta, the five great elements, ether, air, fire, water and earth.

The gunas are the qualities of the mind[1] – sattva, rajas and tamas. Sattva is purity, rajas is the eternal search, whereas tamas is darkness or earthiness. Tamas is the world into which the soul incarnates; it gives birth to the pancha maha bhutas, which control our senses.

The right harmony between purusha and prakriti is the pure consciousness. When this consciousness comes into contact with ahankara, the individual ego, the balance of prakriti is disturbed, the consciousness loses its subtle qualities and becomes more and more under the control of the gross. The gross quality is the guna of tamas and this guna controls the five great elements, which in turn creates our senses and desires.

---

1.   More on gunas in *The Essentials of Vedic Astrology* Chapter 1.

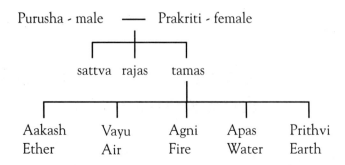

The birth of an individual upsets the universal harmony and we each reflect this disturbed quality. Panchanga shows the quality of consciousness, the outer and inner light we bring to earth. The light of the panchanga is also controlled by the five great elements, one element each controlling one of the limbs of the panchanga.

Purusha and Prakriti – the Eternal and the Changeable

Purusha is the eternal soul, unconscious, everlasting and static, it does not change. Prakriti is nature, forever changing and evolving. Prakriti reflects our unfinished desires and goals. To mature and to complete the unfulfilled karma, the soul has to be incarnated on earth. In the realm of the eternal (purusha) no further spiritual progress can be made; the soul remains at the level it was when it returned to the eternal. To reach the state of moksha, the soul has to be born on earth and come again under the control of the changing, shifting environment of prakriti; it is prakriti that rules the life on earth. The eternal connection between purusha and prakriti suggests that our changeable nature is directly connected to the eternal one. All souls are eternal and divine; only life on earth is changeable.

The Pancha Maha Bhuta, The Five Great Elements –
The Sheaths to the Pure Consciousness

Pancha means five, *maha* is great and *bhuta* is element. *Bhuta* comes from the word Bhu that means the earth. Bhuta is what is formed from the earth or experienced during the earthly birth. It has several other meanings – a primary substance, the true state of the soul, the real nature or the way that worldly issues control the spiritual ones. The pancha maha bhuta are the five primary elements that influence our physical body and also sheath the eternal consciousness. They are also known as the *Pancha Maha Tattvas*. Tattva is another name for bhuta specially when applied to the physical. Normally the elements are written as one word *Panchamahabhuta* but for easier understanding I have split them into three words – pancha maha bhuta. The five great elements are:

Aakash	Ether
Vayu	Air
Agni	Fire
Apas	Water
Prithvi	Earth

The knowledge of these five great elements is essential to understanding panchanga as well as the natal chart.

The Pancha Maha Bhuta

The consciousness manifested into five different elements – ether, air, fire, water and earth. Ether was the primary element, which was created from the vibrations of the sound of Aum. When this ethereal element began to move, it created air, which is ether in action, and created friction which in turn created heat. The heat created light and from light came the fire element. The fire dissolved some of ether's elements, which liquefied and became water. Water solidified to form earth. Ether created the four elements of air, fire, water and earth.

Earth is matter and in matter exists all organic (vegetable, animal and human) and inorganic (the minerals) bodies. The final element of earth is born by the combination of all elements, and all these elements exist within us. Pancha maha bhuta are reflected in the panchanga.

Pancha Maha Bhuta and the Planets

Maharishi Parashara has devoted Chapter 78 *Ath Panchamahabhuta Adhyaya,* in Brihat Parashar Hora Shastra[2] to the five great elements. In Verse Two, he writes:

> The planets Mars, Mercury, Jupiter, Venus, Saturn rule Fire, Earth, Ether, Water and Air.

---

2.   *Brihat Parashar Hora Shastra,* Translated by Girish Chand Sharma, published by Sagar Publications, India.

Mars, Mercury, Jupiter, Venus and Saturn express the practical reality of our life, and their strength or weakness in the chart will show which mahabhuta is at its strongest. The dashas of the planets will also reflect their bhuta. The moment the soul is born, it comes under the influence of these elements. The strength or weakness of these planets indicates our successes and failures.

The Moon has the secondary rulership of the water element and Sun of Fire. Sun and Moon also control the energy of their bhuta. The Sun's transits can control the fire whereas the Moon's transit can raise or depress the water element. Rahu's element is air and Ketu is fire so they influence their respective bhuta in a more shadowy way. During an eclipse the air, fire and water elements are disturbed by the nodes, therefore it is more difficult to achieve inner balance at that time. Also Rahu and Ketu keep the soul attached to issues of this world and the past and unless we learn to transcend their influence, the soul remains caught in its desires and needs.

Bhuta – Element	Planet	Secondary Influences
Aakash – Ether	Jupiter	
Vayu – Air	Saturn	Rahu
Agni – Fire	Mars	Sun, Ketu
Apas – Water	Venus	Moon
Prithvi – Earth	Mercury	

According to Parashara, when these bhuta become purified, they give a special quality to the individual, which is identifiable even without knowing their birth chart. He calls it the aura of the bhuta. The person appears to radiate an aura of happiness and their skin glows in a special way that makes then appear contented and young despite their years. As the aura of a bhuta develops, it gives special characteristics and skills too. While you want most of the bhutas to rise, vayu (Saturn, Rahu) is the only one that needs controlling as it takes away from the gloss and happiness by promoting nervousness and fear. This makes a person appear gaunt, depressed and older than their years.

The strong planets will help their bhuta while the dasha usually promotes the bhuta of its ruler.

Panchanga and the Great Elements

The panchanga shows how the pancha maha bhuta are established within the psychological fibre of the individual. Whether the mind will be able to harmonize the maha bhuta or get submerged in its needs is the story of the panchanga. It shows how we use these mahabhutas and how far are they obscuring our light. The bhuta in a natal chart shows how pure consciousness is caught in the play of maya or the illusionary world, whereas the daily panchanga shows the changing quality of prakriti that affects our nature.

Bhuta	Panchanga
Aakash	Nitya Yoga
Vayu	Nakshatra
Agni	Dina
Apas	Tithi
Prithvi	Karana

1.   **Dina connects to Agni.** Dina shows the energy, activity and physical powers of an individual.

2.   **Nakshatra connects to Vayu.** The nakshatra deals with communication, thoughts, mentality and prana. It also shows the mind of the individual and how it fluctuates daily. The need to be in contact, learning about detachment, and the soul's desires all are within the nakshatra. Vayu can be destructive if not properly channelled, so the correct use of the mind through its birth nakshatra can create a highly constructive individual while the wrong use of the mind can destroy its peace and create stress and a negative atmosphere.

3.   **The Tithi connects to Apas.** Tithi shows our need and ability for relationships, emotions, sexuality and temperament. Tithi compatibility is an area to watch for in all associations.

4.   **Karana connects to Prithvi.** Karana will indicate how we create our karma; what actions we take in life. It reflects stability and consistency, kriyamana karma.

5.   **Yoga connects to Aakash.** It shows what protection and blessings we have in life; our sense of security and happiness.

Keeping the panchamahabhuta in mind, the lords of the panchanga and the quality they express are as follows:

Panchanga	Mahabhuta	Planets	Qualities
Dina	Agni	Mars	Energy
Nakshatra	Vayu	Saturn	Communication
Tithi	Apas	Venus	Relationships
Karana	Prithvi	Mercury	Stability
Yoga	Aakash	Jupiter	Protection

Panchanga is primarily connected to the light of the Sun and the Moon and how the five great elements influence this light. The Sun and Moon do not come under the control of the five great elements but show the evolution and level of development of the elements.

The Five Great Elements, Senses and Desires

These elements control our organs of desire, emotions and senses. They can keep us grounded in gross reality. They represent the soul's complete involvement in the world of matter.

Each bhuta has a planetary ruler, which is connected to a particular sense and its sense organ. It also has an organ of action. Senses are known as *Indriyan* after Indra, the God of all Senses. Indra fell victim to his sensory desires by having an affair with Gantama's wife Ahilya. He was cursed and only through 1000 years of tapasya (austerity) did he regain his balance and receive forgiveness for his transgressions. Jnanendriyas are the sense organs and the Karmendriyas are the work organs.

Bhuta Element	Graha Planet	Indriya Sense	Jnanendriyas Sense organ	Karmendriyas Work organ
Aakash	Jupiter	Hearing	Ear	Mouth (speech)
Vayu	Saturn	Touch	Skin	Hands
Agni	Mars	Sight	Eyes	Feet and lags
Apas	Venus	Taste	Tongue	Genitals
Prithvi	Mercury	Smell	Nose	Anus

The Unending Cycle of Desires

The senses create desires and the desires demand to be fulfilled. The lack of fulfillment of the desires is the main cause of unhappiness, a never-ending hunger, the more you feed desire the greater it becomes. It is referred to as fire of desire in the Vedic texts. This is not the pure fire of a yogi or a spiritual aspirant but the uncontrolled fire of an individual whose desires dominate their life. The Vedas says that if you feed this fire it becomes bigger and bigger, devouring all you give it and still wanting more until it becomes all-consuming. It can envelop an individual and make them lose control of their life. This never ending cycle of desire is represented by the five elements on a gross level and the real soul is completely hidden by it.

The birth chart indicates its strength or weakness through the planets, which can either give us access to heaven and amrita, or deny it. Most of us hover between one and the other with small glimpses of heaven, along with many doses of deprivation and denial. The panchanga shows the light or lack of it from which we can assess the level of our involvement with the gross world.

The wise person understands that the statuary lesson of desires is to control them. When Indra, the god of the senses allowed them to empower his good judgement, he had to spend many lifetimes paying for the fallout. Sacred texts are not against the incarnating soul enjoying its senses and fulfilling its desires; what they warn against is allowing the desires to get out of control and let them rule one's life.

Chakras – The Transformation of the Great Elements from Gross to Subtle

The pancha maha bhuta are linked to the subtle body through their control of the chakras. Chakras or wheels are psychic centers of the bodies. Chakras do not exist in matter but they correspond to certain areas of our physical body. They also let us know how we can truly make the connection between the visible and the invisible. The chakras are where we connect to our astral power and are doorways to the higher self.

All the functions of the body, nervous, digestive, circulatory, respiratory, genito-urinary etc. are under the control of the elements. Wherever there is an interlacing of several nerves, arteries and veins, that centre is called a *plexus* of the physical body and a *chakra* in the spiritual one. Although there are many chakras, there are seven main ones:

1.   Sahasrara – crown chakra
2.   Ajna – third eye
3.   Vishuddhi – throat chakra
4.   Anahata – heart chakra
5.   Manipura – solar plexus chakra
6.   Swadhisthana – sacral chakra
7.   Muladhara – base chakra

The two higher chakras, Sahasrara and Ajna are beyond the control of the elements. Sahasrara deals with the *atma*, the soul which is beyond the pancha maha bhuta but its desires are projected through the prakriti.

Ajna Chakra deals with *mahat* and *chitta*, *manas* and *buddhi*: mind and intellect on the higher level. It controls the lower chakras but for those individuals on the upward path, it can bring total harmony and open the third eye. It helps us to look beyond our earthly restrictions. Ajna chakra can influence the elements but is free of their control.

Vishuddhi, Anahata, Manipura, Swadhisthana and Muladhara, all come under the influence of the elements. As the soul moves downwards, it comes more and more under the control of the bhuta. When spiritual awareness changes the attitude of the individual, each bhuta must be purified before they can start the upward flow of the spirit again.

Chakras and Pancha Maha Bhuta

Chakras	Element	Quality
Sahasrara – crown	beyond elements	pure consciousness
Ajna – third eye	beyond elements	instinctive thinking
Vishuddhi – throat	Aakash – Ether	knowledge, wisdom
Anahata – heart	Vayu – Air	detachment, spiritual love
Manipura – solar plexus	Agni– Fire	desires, insight, vision
Swadhisthana – sacral	Apas – Water	emotions, sexual needs
Muladhara – base	Prithvi – Earth	practical

The Five Doorways to the Spiritual Heart

> The five breaths prana (fire), vyana (ether), apana (water), samana (earth) and udana (air) are the five doorways to the heart. These doorways are openings to God. They relate to eye, ear, speech, mind and breath. Each of the doorways is controlled by a brahma purusha. These doorkeepers control the gateways to bliss. The entry to heaven is for those who learn to control eye, ear, speech, mind and breath.
>
> Chandogya Upanishad Chapter 3 Section 13

The five doorways are the five chakras from Muladhara to Vishuddhi and the brahma purusha that guards the doorways is one of the five great elements that rule the chakra. The doorways that we need to open are within our subtle mind. They are usually blocked by our physical mind.

The pancha maha bhuta within individuals can work on a purely gross, material level or a highly evolved spiritual level through the chakras. On the gross level it gives rise to all our desires, keeping us acting in a way that creates even more connections to the material life. As the soul gets more caught up in matter and entangled in the physical, the bhuta become the blocks to the doorway of the subtle self, but the moment we start living spiritually the nature of the bhuta changes, and the chakras start working.

The Samkhya philosophy of Maharishi Patanjali detailed in his *Yoga Sutras* deals with the rediscovery of pure consciousness hidden through the process of manifestation by the five great elements. It is through the path of yoga that we are able to reverse the trend of manifestation.

As we learn to operate these wheels within our body our physical life becomes more in tune to our astral needs and we begin to activate our own higher consciousness. Chakras connect the astral with the physical.

Opening of each of the chakras gives a special insight to happiness and bliss as well as the gaining of siddhis (psychic powers to defy destiny and obstructions) and spiritual knowledge. We begin to retrace the soul back to its source when we learn to connect the base chakra to the crown, in fact as we begin to reconcile our material desires to the spiritual, we experience supreme bliss or moksha.

Panchanga and the Chakras

Panchanga gives more understanding of the chakras as each limb controls a chakra and therefore has say in how the doorway can be accessed. The blocks or strengths also relate to how we learn to operate on the subtle level of the chakras. As we begin to study the panchanga we understand how the person is caught up in the play of materialism, but also learn that by using the panchanga we can change the quality from gross to subtle.

Panchanga and the Chakras

Chakras	Element	Panchanga
Vishuddhi – throat	Aakash – Ether	Nitya Yoga
Anahata – heart	Vayu – Air	Nakshatra
Manipura – solar plexus	Agni – Fire	Dina
Swadhisthana – sacral	Apas – Water	Tithi
Muladhara – base	Prithvi – Earth	Karana

Conflicting Bhuta

Agni (fire) and apas (water) are conflicting elements. Fire can heat up water and water puts out fire. So wherever these two elements co-exist you can expect problems.

Vayu can create storms for both agni and apas. It can make the agni rage out of control or blow it out. It can create emotional storms for apas. Neither apas or agni have control over vayu, which is why vayu is so difficult to handle. No one can control it but itself. When it rises it is negative, whereas a calm vayu is good.

Prithvi nurtures and supports all the bhuta and aakash protects them. It is only the inner three elements that can interact negatively with each other.

The Gandanta, the karmic knot that is created at the junction points between Cancer-Leo, Scorpio-Sagittarius and Pisces-Aries, is due to the shift from water to fire elements. This is a karmic position where the soul is thrown from the world of apas immediately into the agni. This creates many problems as the soul struggles to deal with the conflicting elements.

The Five Great Elements and their Various Influences

Aakash – Ether
Ruled by Jupiter
Chakra – Vishuddhi
The limb of the panchanga is Nitya yoga

Ether is related to sound, it affects hearing and speech, the ear and mouth. Jupiter rules this element. Vishuddhi is the chakra. Vishuddhi chakra has the ability to purify the poisons. Ether protects the world from the negative side of the other elements; those with a prominent ether element can be wise, knowledgeable, diplomatic and intuitive, with the ability to hear what was left unsaid. They will be protective of others.

The aura of an evolved aakash gives a beautiful voice, eloquence and such sweetness that people find solace just from listening to their voice.

The Nitya yoga in panchanga shows whether or not we feel protected and supported in life and can deal with its challenges. Some of the yogas are complex and tend to create insecurity and make the individual feel unprotected. More will be explained on Nitya yoga in Chapter 7.

If Jupiter is debilitated (Capricorn) or badly placed, it makes this element defective or under-active in the natal chart, thus creating an imbalance.

Vayu – Air
Ruled by Saturn
Chakra – Anahata
The limb of the panchanga is nakshatras

Vayu relates to the sense of touch. The skin is the sensory organ of touch and the hand is the physical organ. The chakra is anahata. Anahata deals with pure love and detachment. Saturn allows the person to be detached from illusionary love and to love others for what they are, not who we want them to be. A prominent air element will be nervous, charitable, kind, angry, destructive, difficult to please, communicative, productive and majestic.

Vayu is the element of movement. The evolved vayu is not easy and its aura shows stress, worry and depression. This means that we should restrict movement – physically and emotionally. Too much vayu will aggravate the mind and once it rises is usually difficult to calm down; it soon becomes a destructive force. Usually when vayu rises in a person they can become prone to disease, poverty, and make unwise decisions due to emotional instability and depression. In my view if individuals learn to control vayu through meditation, yoga and chanting, they can also be at peace with themselves, willing to face any hurdle with equanimity; wise through life experience.

In panchanga, the nakshatras indicate how we use the vayu. The nakshatras are connected to the mind and therefore a troubled mind shows a troubled vayu element. Birth in a difficult nakshatra or the Moon being in a troubled position can make us feel emotionally imbalanced.

Saturn rules this element. Saturn in Aries or in an otherwise negative position in the chart will create problems with mobility and bring anger from frustration.

Agni – Fire
Ruled by Mars
Chakra – Manipura
The limb of the panchanga is dina

Agni is heat, light and colour and is related to vision. It rules the eye, the sight, the sense of direction as well as the decisive action of walking. Eyes direct the feet to walk – blind people usually walk without direction. The chakra is manipura, our personal gem. A strong fire element gives a robust appetite, an active nature, and a courageous, dominating personality. These people can overindulge their senses through sex, eating, domination and sensual living. They are usually overbearing, hard to handle personalities. If you come too close to them, you can get burnt. They can be selfish.

Mars rules fire and the Sun controls the fire element by its seasons. The Sun's heat during the summer will ignite the fire bhuta whereas it will keep it calm during winter. The Sun transits towards and away from the earth – dakshin ayana and uttara ayana, the differing lengths of the days of the Sun all contribute to control over the fire bhuta. The seasonal effect of the Sun will have a major influence on this bhuta.

The aura of an evolved agni will make one shine like gold, eyes full of purity, loving, happy and warm. These people treat everyone equally and with love and achieve success in all they do. Everything they touch is gold, *sarva siddhi* – talented all round. They can acquire unimaginable wealth which they will use for good causes.

It rules the dina in panchanga. Dina is the day of the week. You need to study the ruler of the day of birth further to see how you use this element.

The Sun rules this element. A weak Mars or Sun will block this bhuta and tend to promote the negative qualities of agni. It can give a poor metabolism and create weight problems too.

Apas – Water
Ruled by Venus
Chakra – Swadhisthana
The limb of the panchanga is tithi

Apas reflects taste and the tongue. The tongue is symbolically connected to the genitals   and in Ayurveda the genitals are considered the lower tongue. As the body is over 85% water, this is a most important element. Keeping this element pure and flowing goes a long way to creating emotional harmony. Water is kept pure by right emotions, involvement in committed and secure sexual relationships and good food. One of the easiest ways to pollute the water element is through multiple, unhappy sexual relationships, jealousy, envy and lack of good food (fast foods, foods cooked in anger, old foods). The chakra is swadhisthana, which means your own place.

Water people are polite, caring, friendly, happy, creative, soft, learned and educated. They will help others willingly and be a soft touch for emotional stories. They can be moody and temperamental. Their body radiates beauty.

The aura of an evolved apas gives good health, grace, emotional stability and happiness through good food and relationships.

In panchanga, tithi is the limb controlled by the water element. There are certain tithis that naturally have difficulty in relating. Tithis will also reflect our emotions.

Venus rules this element. Just as the Moon controls the tides of the oceans, it controls the tides within us by its waxing and waning process. If the Moon is in Scorpio or Venus in Virgo, this element will be out of balance. These people can be possessive and bitter, and they will show a distinct lack of happiness. The water element can shift according to the lunar phases, and knowing how to deal with this helps override any weakness in the chart.

Prithvi – Earth
Ruled by Mercury
Chakra – Muladhara
The limb of the panchanga is karana

Life is possible because earth holds all living and non-living substances on its surface and within. The sense of smell is related to earth. The nose is its organ. The nose is symbolically connected to the anus – the organ of excretion. Bad breath is usually caused by constipation. The chakra is muladhara – the support of both spiritual and material life.

The senses can easily dominate if prithvi is strong. These people enjoy luxury, they are practical and like to live in comfortable surroundings. They will be powerful, forgiving, and usually have a strong voice. They can get used to their surroundings, craving security and a settled life.

In panchanga, prithvi rules karana. Karana shows how we create the karma of this life, through our work, choices and free will. Karana also shows the profession.

Mercury rules earth. Mercury retrogrades three times a year, and it becomes combust at least six times a year. This shows the unstable nature of life on earth. Although prithvi represents continuity and solidity, it is not easy to achieve the steadiness of the prithvi bhuta. Any problems with the natal Mercury will indicate problems with being practical, especially Mercury in Pisces which looks beyond life on earth and wants to explore higher realms. The earth of Mercury mixing with the water of Pisces can create muddy water and confuse the intellect and a weak Mercury can create insecurities too. We have to be aware of the constantly changing nature of Mercury in transit and this can create problems with the prithvi bhuta even if there is none in the natal chart.

The aura of an evolved prithvi gives security, wealth and happiness, a person who is well groomed and spiritual. These people honour their time on earth but are also conscious of the need to improve and search the higher self. One of the qualities of an evolved prithvi is that the body smells beautiful without the use of any perfumes or deodorants.

Rashi Pancha Maha Bhuta

This is a different classification of the rashi (sign) rulers from the one we are used to. Here the sign takes over the element of its ruler. We should always study this classification alongside the classical one as it gives a further understanding of the rashi qualities. In rashi pancha maha bhuta Scorpio, which is traditionally watery, also reflects the fire element as its ruler Mars is fiery. So Scorpio expresses water and fire.

Libra and Scorpio are the only two signs where the dual elements are in conflict. Libra is water and air, Scorpio is fire and water – both have the capacity to be disturbed. These rashis are in conflict within themselves. Libra will try to find a balance even though they remain emotionally troubled, as vayu will churn up water, the emotions, although water does not effect the vayu. In the complex world of Scorpio, fire makes water hot or burns it out, causing extreme situations within their bhuta. Both Libra and Scorpio lagnas should try very hard to do the bhuta shuddhi and purify themselves; otherwise they can be very troubled.

From the chart below you see that the signs have their own element not necessarily related to their planetary ruler. If you take the planetary ruler's element into account, the signs will have dual elements. Similarly nakshatras have their own elements, which do not reflect the nakshatra of the rasi they are in nor of their ruler. There are some exceptions.

Signs	Ruling planet	Elements from sign	Elements from its ruler	Elements from rashi and its ruler
Aries	Mars	Fire	Fire	Fire – Fire
Taurus	Venus	Earth	Water	Earth – Water
Gemini	Mercury	Air	Earth	Air – Earth
Cancer	Moon	Water	Water	Water – Water
Leo	Sun	Fire	Fire	Fire – Fire
Virgo	Mercury	Earth	Earth	Earth – Earth
Libra	Venus	Air	Water	Air – Water
Scorpio	Mars	Water	Fire	Water – Fire
Sagittarius	Jupiter	Fire	Ether	Fire – Ether
Capricorn	Saturn	Earth	Air	Earth – Air
Aquarius	Saturn	Air	Air	Air – Air
Pisces	Jupiter	Water	Ether	Water – Ether

Rasi and their rulers reflecting similar elements on both levels
Vayu – Aquarius (Saturn and Rahu)
Agni – Aries (Mars), Leo (Sun)
Apas – Cancer (Moon)
Prithvi – Virgo (Mercury)

These signs become concentrated expressions of these bhuta. Planets placed within them become strongly influenced by their bhuta. Aquarius is a pure vayu sign and therefore Aquarius lagna, Moon and Sun have to keep the air element in control both mentally and physically or it can create problems for them. Yoga would be greatly helpful for these people.

3

DINA OR SOLAR DAY

*D*ina means day. A solar day begins at sunrise and ends at sunrise of
the next solar day. There are 360 dina in a solar year, one day for
one degree of the zodiac – this is different from the calendar year we use
today. Different planets rule the days in the week and the name of the
planet is prefixed to *vaar* to give a particular day. Dina connects to the
Sun and therefore to the soul. As the Sun also deals with the vitality of
the body, dina shows the source of energy each soul has for this lifetime.

Dina is the most important component of the panchanga as it is
the primary influence on the soul. The planet that rules the dina has a
lot to say about how the soul feels about this incarnation, what energy it
is going to contribute to running the material world and how the soul
communicates with the world. The physical prowess, health or ill health
and the bhuta that rules all have impact on the prakriti (nature) on the
physical and mental level through doshas and gunas. From Sunday to
Saturday the dina and their planetary rulers are:

1. Ravivaar – Sun's day
2. Somvaar – Moon's day
3. Mangalvaar – Mars' day
4. Buddhvaar – Mercury's day
5. Brihaspativaar or Guruvaar – Jupiter's day
6. Shukravaar – Venus's day
7. Shanivaar – Saturn's day

The dina has four important subdivisions, all of which indicate
how we use our energy and have a direct influence on our health:

Hora – The dina is divided into 24 horas or hours; each lorded by a
different planet.

Maha Bhuta rising and falling – The dina is divided into twelve three-
hour sections where all the mahabhuta rise and fall, so the dina reflects
all the sources of energy and the predominant bhuta that is rising at the
time of birth.

The Rising Guna – The dina is divided into sixteen portions of 1½ hours each. From sunrise each day a different guna is prominent in these sections known as velas. Tamas, sattva and rajas rise and repeat themselves during the day.

Day Nakshatras – Both the day and the night are divided into fifteen parts each; these thirty divisions reflect the thirty tithis. A day runs from sunrise to sunset and a night from sunset to sunrise and the lengths of the divisions depend on the lengths of the days and nights. According to the time of birth, each nakshatra during the day gives indications of our mental energies.

The overall ruler of dina is the Sun, the bhuta ruler is Mars and each dina has its own lordship. The hora lord, the dina nakshatra and the rising mahabhuta modify the dina.

Vedic Day

The vedic day begins at sunrise and ends at sunrise of the next day. For example, in panchanga a Saturday birth will only count as Saturday after sunrise – the time before that belongs to Friday. The dina of the day of birth will be the day of the week on which the Sun rose at a particular place (local time). In effect two people born on the same date may have a different dina according to the place of birth. If the sun rose in UK at 4.30am on Sunday morning on the 1st of June, a birth at 4.25am would count as Saturday, and a birth at 4.35am would count as Sunday. Two people born at the same time in the same country could have a different dina as the Sun may rise earlier at one place than another. This changes the quality of their personalities and their connection with the eternal, as one will inherit Saturn's qualities and the other the Sun's. Most vedic software gives the sunrise time of the place you are born and will also show the panchanga.

The Quality of Dina Bhuta is Agni

Agni was the primary principle through which the gods communicated with the earth and agni feeds from the offerings given to gods by humans. Agni wants the soul to act in the voice of God, to dedicate all its actions and karma to the gods as explained by *Sri Krishna* in *Bhagawad Gita*. If all the actions are thus dedicated there is no need to worry about getting any negative effects of karma. But Mars as the ruler of agni tends to

make actions more selfish and related to fulfilling the desires of the ego. Everyone wants personal rewards for their actions and this creates disturbance in the agni, not allowing the fire to burn cleanly. If actions are devoted to doing the right thing without hope for reward, the agni becomes purified and comes back under the control of the Sun, the co-ruler and the controller of agni. The fire of pure karma does not leave dross behind to be dealt with in another day or another lifetime.

The Role of Sun and Mars

If the Sun and Mars are strong in the natal chart, they will support all the dina. Always remember the difference between the motivation of the Sun and Mars: The Sun wants to work in accordance with the soul's desires while Mars wants to work according to its individuality, and will therefore be more selfish. Depending on their strength or weakness, Mars or the Sun will indicate which planet has the bigger say in how the energy is used. A weak Sun will not be able to follow the spiritual path if Mars is strong and taking a selfish stand. A weak Mars can either misuse its energy or take the unethical path. A weakness of either Mars or the Sun can make a person unfocused, not knowing how to use their energy. There can be a lack of physical strength, which blocks them from doing things even if they want to. The aspects of the Sun and Mars will further refine the effects of these planets. The dina or hora rulers bring their own influences on the primary energy of the Sun and Mars, with the dina lords sometimes so strong that they make a person initially confused on their path.

Hora

Dina is further divided into 24 horas; hourly divisions of the day. *Hora* means an hour. Divide the duration of the day – sunrise to sunset – into twelve equal parts, and the duration of the night – from sunset to sunrise – into twelve equal parts also. These 24 subdivisions are known as hora. Unlike the 60-minute hour, the time of each hora varies according to the exact period between sunrise and sunset, or sunset and sunrise. The only time the horas reflect the exact hour is at the equinoxes when sunrise and sunset around the world is uniform, otherwise horas expand or contract according to the rising and setting of the Sun and the length of the hora will differ during the day and the night.

Hora Table

Hora	Sunday	Monday	Tues	Wed	Thurs	Friday	Sat
1	Sun	Moon	Mars	Mercury	Jupiter	Venus	Saturn
2	Venus	Saturn	Sun	Moon	Mars	Mercury	Jupiter
3	Mercury	Jupiter	Venus	Saturn	Sun	Moon	Mars
4	Moon	Mars	Mercury	Jupiter	Venus	Saturn	Sun
5	Saturn	Sun	Moon	Mars	Mercury	Jupiter	Venus
6	Jupiter	Venus	Saturn	Sun	Moon	Mars	Mercury
7	Mars	Mercury	Jupiter	Venus	Saturn	Sun	Moon
8	Sun	Moon	Mars	Mercury	Jupiter	Venus	Saturn
9	Venus	Saturn	Sun	Moon	Mars	Mercury	Jupiter
10	Mercury	Jupiter	Venus	Saturn	Sun	Moon	Mars
11	Moon	Mars	Mercury	Jupiter	Venus	Saturn	Sun
12	Saturn	Sun	Moon	Mars	Mercury	Jupiter	Venus
13	Jupiter	Venus	Saturn	Sun	Moon	Mars	Mercury
14	Mars	Mercury	Jupiter	Venus	Saturn	Sun	Moon
15	Sun	Moon	Mars	Mercury	Jupiter	Venus	Saturn
16	Venus	Saturn	Sun	Moon	Mars	Mercury	Jupiter
17	Mercury	Jupiter	Venus	Saturn	Sun	Moon	Mars
18	Moon	Mars	Mercury	Jupiter	Venus	Saturn	Sun
19	Saturn	Sun	Moon	Mars	Mercury	Jupiter	Venus
20	Jupiter	Venus	Saturn	Sun	Moon	Mars	Mercury
21	Mars	Mercury	Jupiter	Venus	Saturn	Sun	Moon
22	Sun	Moon	Mars	Mercury	Jupiter	Venus	Saturn
23	Venus	Saturn	Sun	Moon	Mars	Mercury	Jupiter
24	Mercury	Jupiter	Venus	Saturn	Sun	Moon	Mars

The order of the horas is dependent upon the distance of the planets from Earth. Saturn is the furthest away, then Jupiter, Mars, Sun, Venus, Mercury and Moon. The first hora rising is always the ruler of the dina. For Sunday the first hora will be Sun, the second hora will be Venus, which is closer to Earth, then Mercury and then the Moon. After the Moon hora it goes back to Saturn, the furthest away from the Earth, and the sequence works inwards again.

While hora is more precise as it shows the exact influence of the hour of birth, it remains subordinate to the dina and modifies the influence of the dina. Dina is the energy in the body; hora shows how we use the energy. Influences will vary according to the strength of the hora lord. If it is stronger than the dina lord, the hora lord will try to dominate. The type of influence depends on the nature of the hora lord and its planetary relationship with the dina lord. Conflicting bhuta of the dina and hora lord can lead to a misuse of energy. If it is an enemy planet and negative to the dina lord, then it creates an emotional imbalance and a disconnection with the soul, and can take the soul off its chosen pathway.

Dina versus Hora

The dina we are born under will show how we act in life, the karma we create and what planetary energy we have inherited at birth. The hora is how we use the energy and modify it for better or for worse. These influences on the soul are reflected in our personalities.

Hora modifies the dina. If both the hora and dina lords are the same they express the pure quality of that planet. Its position in the birth chart will show how this is expressed. Any weakness or strength to both will strongly influence the energy.

When analysing dina and hora, think of physical energy, the verve, the enthusiasm for life, how we are going to direct our lives. As each action has a reaction, the true way of putting energy to good use is to focus it in the right direction, but in conflicting dina and hora lordships the differing bhuta do not make for an even playing field. As dina is the communication with the gods and the soul, we need to be conscious of doing good actions to keep the doorways open. Misguided actions only serve to cut our connection with the higher self.

You should study the natural planetary relationships between the planets to understand how the dina and hora relate to each other. Also study the position of the dina and hora lords and their relationship in the chart.

The Prakriti of the Dina Lord

Prakriti is nature and the elementary principle on which the sustenance of the body depends. There are three body types based on the biological humours or dhatus, known as vata, pitta and kapha. These types of nature govern the biological, psychological and physiological functions of the body, mind and consciousness. When they are in balance we are healthy. When one or the other predominates, it creates illness and becomes a dosha. These body types form the basis of Ayurveda.

Each dina ruler has its own prakriti. This plays a vital role in understanding the health of an individual:

Prakriti	Planet
Pitta	Mars, Sun
Vata	Saturn
Kapha	Moon, Jupiter, Venus

Mercury can reflect all the three types. Its nature depends on the planet it conjuncts.

When these three states get into a state of imbalance, they become a dosha. The Sanskrit word *dosha* means fault or weakness. This term is used in Ayurveda to find the weakness in the nature of man that causes diseases when aggravated. The body constitution is governed at birth. One of the most important contributions is made by the dina lord, which indicates the quality of your nature. The quality of the lord of the dina in the birth chart will indicate whether this nature is in balance or out of balance.

Guna of the Day Lord and the Guna Rising

Consciousness has a balance of the three mental qualities, sattva, rajas and tamas, collectively called gunas. Sattva is the illuminating, pure quality, rajas is the quality of mobility, activity and achievement, and tamas is the dark restraining materialistic quality.

Each planet has its own guna and each time of birth has its own guna. Depending on the dina of birth, the mental energy of the soul would first reflect the guna of the dina lord and the quality of the rising guna:

Planet	Guna
Sun	Sattva
Moon	Sattva
Mars	Tamas
Mercury	Triguni*
Jupiter	Sattva
Venus	Rajas
Saturn	Tamas

*Mercury can reflect any of the gunas depending on the sign and planet it is placed with.

Vela Table

Velas → Day ↓	1	2	3	4	5	6	7	8	9	10	11	12	13	14	15	16
Sun	T	S	R	T	S	R	T	S	R	T	S	R	T	S	R	T
Mon	S	R	T	S	R	T	S	R	T	S	R	T	S	R	T	S
Tues	R	T	S	R	T	S	R	T	S	R	T	S	R	T	S	R
Wed	T	S	R	T	S	R	T	S	R	T	S	R	T	S	R	T
Thur	S	R	T	S	R	T	S	R	T	S	R	T	S	R	T	S
Fri	R	T	S	R	T	S	R	T	S	R	T	S	R	T	S	R
Sat	T	S	R	T	S	R	T	S	R	T	S	R	T	S	R	T

According to Jataka Parijata[1]; tamas, sattva and rajas rise during the day for 1½ hours at a time and this cycle repeats throughout the day. The segments are known as satovela (sattvic time), rajovela (rajasic time) and tamovela (tamasic time).

The day is divided into 16 portions of 1½ hours each. From sunrise each day a different guna is prominent in these sections known as velas. Beginning with Sunday when the first vela is tamas at sunrise for 1½ hours, the next is sattva and the third is rajas, and these repeat themselves till the last one is tamas again. On Monday the sun rises with sattva.

Day	First vela at sunrise
Sunday	Tamas
Monday	Sattva
Tuesday	Raja
Wednesday	Tamas
Thursday	Sattva
Friday	Rajas
Saturday	Tamas

Satovela persons are eloquent, dutiful, wise, spiritual, devout, preserving, pure, bountiful, lustrous, truthful and without enemies.

Rajovela persons are famous, happy, wealthy, strong, romantic, passionate but not close to their kin. They are always searching so they can get burnt out easily.

Tamovela persons can be full of desires. This can create unhappiness and health problems through their fixed natures and inability to change. However they can be steadfast and enduring.

---

1.   Jataka Parijata Book Two, Adhyaya IX , Velaphalam, 123-125 Shlokas.

Dina at Birth

Sunday
Ruler – Sun, prakriti is pitta, guna is sattva

These people are brave, strong, firm, generous, bountiful, energetic, bright, loyal, steady, and visionary. They are popular and have many friends yet can be loners. If the Sun is weak in the rashi chart, it can make them rigid, arrogant, aggressive and dominating. As the Sun is the ruler of agni and represents the overall energy and it rules the dina as well, its weakness or strength can create a double impact – weak becomes weaker and strong becomes stronger. Those with weak Suns should work with remedial measures to strengthen the Sun and follow the path of Ayurveda, yoga and proper food to invigorate the physical and the mental. Their prakriti (nature) is pitta or fiery, they have good robust health. The sattva guna gives them an idealistic attitude.

Monday
Ruler – Moon, prakriti is kapha, guna is sattva

These people are nurturing, flexible, learned, peaceful, well spoken, supportive, calm, passionate, and happy to take a secondary position. They need the support of others. They can be commitment phobic. If the Moon is weak, it can give dependency, negativity, unreliability, a lack of peace of mind, agitation and fickleness. Life can appear insecure and uncertain. They may promise you anything but are not always able to fulfil their promises, so are deemed unreliable. The sattvik mentality makes them idealistic, always working for the good of others. Although they have a kapha nature, the perpetual movement of the Moon can give it an added vata quality.

Tuesday
Ruler – Mars, prakriti is pitta, guna is tamas

These people are confident, courageous, happy to argue and debate, with speech that can be sarcastic, but the heart is pure and they are very loyal and will defend the needy. They can be autocratic, warlike, sporty, and good at leadership. A weak Mars makes them energy-wasting and unsure, with honey tongues on the surface but grudges held within. They are not good at taking command and look for support. A weak Mars will have a double impact like the Sun as it rules the bhuta of the dina and the dina of birth. Physical health should be taken care of through the practice of yoga, Ayurveda and good food. The individual must learn to use their energy wisely and keep focused on their main aims otherwise they can waste their talents. Mars is fiery by nature and although the active Mars appears to be rajasic, the mentality is tamas as it can remain practical and down to earth.

Wednesday
Ruler – Mercury, prakriti is tridosha, guna is rajas
These people are well spoken, wealthy, attractive, charming, dextrous and forever multi-tasking. Being flexible in mind and body makes them intellectually powerful, learned, good at appreciating art, plus good at yoga, gymnastics and other sports where agility is required. They have excellent business skills and can be good at motivating people and getting the best out of them as they recognise and appreciate others' qualities. If Mercury is weak they become unreliable, prone to lying, fickle, speaking what others want to hear and not very practical. They remain good at writing and the arts. Their nature is changeable and they do not conform to any specific body type. Their nature is rajasic, always searching for answers.

Thursday
Ruler – Jupiter, prakriti is kapha, guna is sattva
These people are blessed with virtuous qualities. They are spiritual, knowledgeable, wealthy in mind and spirit, generous, attractive, always receiving gifts and presents, honoured by the state, popular, loved by people in power and appreciated by their gurus. A weak Jupiter can make the individual calculating and miserly, a show-off who appears spiritual but does not follow the path; unhappy, unappreciated and bitter. Their kapha nature makes them calm in a crisis, but can also give a tendency to gain weight. They are sattvic and their motivation and thinking is usually pure.

Friday
Ruler – Venus, prakriti is kapha, guna is rajas
These people are beautiful, handsome, liking to wear white, with a rare intelligence and an artistic eye for beauty and creativity. They will try to

follow the good path and are worldly yet secretive. If Venus is weak they can become super critical, and spoil their ability to admire beauty. A weak Venus still gives them the ability to appreciate beauty but they will set such high standards that none can live up to them, and so they feel perpetually unhappy.

Saturday
Ruler – Saturn, prakriti is vata, guna is tamas
These people are responsible, hardworking, shouldering all responsibility, workaholic, stoic and able to face pain and sorrow. Their beauty can get marred by a physical mark or blemish or by life's circumstances, (this can be reflected in their dour, pessimistic expression), but they look and feel younger as they grow older. Feeling old or ugly can mar their youth, which may not be the reality but is just how they feel. Hunger for success makes them work hard but if Saturn is weak they can be dissatisfied and make no effort to improve their life. They can feel negative, bitter, angry, bad tempered, greedy, irresponsible, impulsive, become prematurely old and lack good health. Saturn's vata nature makes them always on the move and they can waste energy through too much worry. The guna is tamas, so they may remain in unhappy situations too long. Their attachment to the material can sometimes cause them pain.

The Hora at Birth
Sun hora: This hora wants to be strong and powerful and help the person find their own place in the world. They will act royally with energy, strength, courage and a sunny nature. They aspire for positions of strength, but problems can arise if the dina lord is Saturn, which oppresses the Sun's vitality. A sunnier positive disposition is possible if the Sun and Saturn are well placed to each other. If the dina lord is combusted by the Sun, the hora lord can take over the energy of the dina too. Mercury transits close to the Sun and is therefore most likely to be combust. The Monday and Friday dina lords' bhuta is water and it conflicts with the fire bhuta of the Sun. The fire and water elements create a hot and cold personality, sometimes too heated, sometimes totally cold or passive. They do not know how to use their energy properly and this can make them hard to understand. Monday with a Sun hora will be emotionally hot and cold whereas Friday with a Sun hora can become sexually so.

Moon hora: These people will be intuitive in the way they use their energy. They will be caring and helpful, keeping on gathering information but not always using their wealth of knowledge. Nurturing ideas and creativity is their talent and they must be careful not to waste their energy. If the dina is Friday, both the dina lord and the hora lord are water elements, and can become too emotional and sensitive; their desires and needs dominating their life unless they are careful. A Moon hora will soften the Sun, but one must be mindful it does not extinguish the strong qualities of the Sun. As the Moon debilitates Mars[2], those born on its hora on Tuesday should take care not to soften Mars's impact too much. This can also make the elements conflict with the person sometimes showing the fire quality and at other times water, or a mixture of both.

Mars hora: This hora gives confidence, organisational ability and a logical way of thinking and expressing oneself, plus courage and the need to be in control. A Mars hora on Monday and Friday will bring conflicting elements together; on Friday this leads to excessive passions whereas on Monday the emotions can get out of control. A Mars hora on Monday can create a stronger personality and is easier to handle than on Friday as the Moon and Mars are friends and Venus and Mars are not. A Mars hora on Saturday is also difficult to handle as Saturn is cautious by nature and Mars more adventurous. Also Mars debilitates Saturn[3] and the combination can easily lead to frustrations and a misuse of energy as both may be using their strengths in opposite directions. A Mars hora can also be difficult on Wednesday as Mercury and Mars are inimical to each other. Mercury thinks and Mars acts, so Mars will encourage Mercury to act without thinking. If this can be resolved it can make them come alive as Mars will help achieve ambitions.

Mercury hora: These people will find many areas to use their talents. They must not spread themselves too thinly or they will be doing too many things but achieving less. They need to focus. Writing, business and communications are their skills. A Mercury hora will be difficult on

---

2.   Mars is debilitated in Cancer, which is ruled by the Moon.
3.   Saturn is debilitated in Aries, which is ruled by Mars.

Monday, Tuesday and Friday. On Monday both the dina and hora lord would be connected to the mind, but as Mercury is inimical to the Moon it will always question its intuition. Mercury and the Moon can both be fickle, so in a worst case scenario this is an extremely indecisive situation, both lacking commitment. On a Tuesday Mercury questions Mars, which can again create confusion in how to use talents properly. As regards Friday, Venus and Mercury are friends, yet Mercury's sign Virgo debilitates Venus so this combination has to be carefully dealt with. This can be a magical combination or a difficult one. The practical more earthy side of Mercury can make Venus lose purity and muddy the water element. A Mercury hora must support Venus through right thinking and right ideas and not be overly critical of its qualities. On Sunday, Mercury can be a good hora as long as Mercury is not combust by the Sun[4], otherwise the qualities of Mercury will remain absent while those of the Sun dominate.

Jupiter hora: These people will deal with knowledge one way or another. They can be writers, teachers, consultants, gurus etc., and will try to take wise steps, thinking things through. They will be expansive by nature so have grand ideas with which to expend their energy. A Jupiter hora on Wednesday can be difficult as Jupiter debilitates Mercury[5], and can take away the sharpness of intellect, though it does add an extra dimension from a spiritual point of view. Mercury usually wants evidence for everything and a Jupiter hora can infuse them with wisdom and create a different kind of thinking that is not always practical. This can be a good combination for authors, publishers and advisors but not so good for practical purposes. A Jupiter hora is usually a good one to have as it brings its natural beneficence to every dina.

Venus hora: These people will use their energy artistically and creatively with an interest in music or the creative arts. Venus is regarded as a guru so also exudes a talent for counselling and advising. A Venus hora on Sunday is the most difficult as it debilitates the Sun[6], weakening it by encouraging a focus on the pleasures of life and relationships. This is not necessarily a negative thing but the quality of the Sun is to be alone and

---

4.   Mercury transits close to the Sun, therefore is most likely to be combust.
5.   Mercury is debilitated in Pisces, which is ruled by Jupiter.
6.   Sun is debilitated in Libra, a sign ruled by Venus.

strong and Venus encourages dependency. A Venus hora on Tuesday also creates problems as Venus is sensuous and can confuse the logic of Mars. This can make the Mars person addicted to a more comfortable lifestyle where they should naturally be tougher and stronger. As water and fire are inimical to each other, Venus's water confuses the fire of the Sun and Mars. Venus's focus can put out the fire of the Sun and Mars, so this is a tricky balance. On Monday a Venus hora brings more water to the emotional Moon, adding desires to a person who is not well grounded; though this may not be as negative as a Moon hora on Friday as Venus exalts the Moon.[7]

Saturn hora: This hora gives a cautious approach to life and would be good in most cases as Saturn always brings hard work which helps the individual fulfill their ambitions. But Saturn is vayu by nature so can make a person worry unnecessarily. The main principal of vayu is that it must be directed correctly otherwise it can be destructive. Those with a Saturn hora need to give their life a proper direction, then Saturn will be extremely productive regardless of whether he is a friend or foe. Sunday and Thursday-born people can have problems with Saturn horas. The Sun and Saturn are inimical by nature and Saturn will want to trample on the grand solar ideas of how to use their energy. It can make the fire go out of control, encouraging over ambitious and domineering behaviour. If the Saturn hora is used properly, it gives an ability to be humble and hardworking despite any grand ambitions. Saturn also debilitates Jupiter,[8] making this an uncomfortable hora to have on a Thursday. Saturn can restrict Jupiter's generous and expansive nature making these people more calculating and businesslike. But Saturn can also help the Thursday-born achieve whatever they want if they learn to keep their Jupiter quality while using the positive aspects of Saturn.

The Daily Rise and Fall of the Panchamahabhuta
Different bhuta influence different times of the day, rising and falling within three hours. Three hours is an average time, the time of the cycle can change according to the length of the day and night. So in summer,

---

7.   Moon is exalted in Taurus, which is ruled by Venus.
8.   Jupiter is debilitated in Saturn's sign Capricorn.

the day cycles will be longer than the night ones and the reverse in winter. They first go in a direct order known as *arohi* and then in an indirect order known as *avarohi*. This full cycle of three hours includes an upward rising cycle of 90 minutes and a downward cycle of 90 minutes. One set of bhuta takes 90 minutes and then reverses its order. Prithvi time is 6 minutes, apas 12 minutes, agni 18 minutes, vayu 24 minutes and aakash 30 minutes.

Other Factors to be Taken into Consideration

The Cycle of Bhuta

Bhuta	Lord	Time	Sex
Prithvi	Mercury	6 min	Male
Apas	Venus	12 min	Female
	Moon		
Agni	Mars	18 min	Male
	Sun		
Vayu	Saturn	24 min	Female
Aakash	Jupiter	30 min	Male

The three-hour cycle of the rise and fall of the bhuta is also connected to our breath. We tend to breathe out of *ida nadi* (left nostril) for 1½ hours and *pingala nadi* (right nostril) for 1½ hours. Ida is the softer, cooler side of the person and pingala the more aggressive side, so ida would be a falling bhuta and pingala a rising bhuta. Even when one nostril is more dominant, persons conversant with *swara shastra*, the art of reading the breath, can tell which bhuta is more dominant through their breath and sense of smell.

The bhuta, which is connected to you, gives a strong idea of what element is the driving force in your personality. If it is rising it indicates a more determined, action oriented person and if the bhuta is falling it denotes someone more passive.

The changeover times can also have important influences and this can be an important tool for rectifying charts. An astrologer would be able to tell the exact time of birth according to the sex of the individual as certain bhuta are male and others female. A slight shift at changeover

The Three-hour Cycles of the Seven Days

Sunday			
One cycle of 3 hours			
Arohi 1½ hrs		Avrohi 1½ hours	
Bhuta	**min**	**Bhuta**	**Time**
Agni	18	Apas	12
Vayu	24	Prithvi	6
Aakash	30	Aakash	30
Prithvi	6	Vayu	24
Apas	12	Agni	18

Monday			
One cycle of 3 hours			
Arohi 1½ hrs		Avrohi 1½ hours	
Bhuta	**min**	**Bhuta**	**Time**
Apas	12	Prithvi	6
Agni	18	Aakash	30
Vayu	24	Vayu	24
Aakash	30	Agni	18
Prithvi	6	Apas	12

Tuesday			
One cycle of 3 hours			
Arohi 1½ hrs		Avrohi 1½ hours	
Bhuta	**min**	**Bhuta**	**Time**
Agni	18	Apas	12
Vayu	24	Prithvi	6
Aakash	30	Aakash	30
Prithvi	6	Vayu	24
Apas	12	Agni	18

Wednesday			
One cycle of 3 hours			
Arohi 1½ hrs		Avrohi 1½ hours	
Bhuta	**min**	**Bhuta**	**Time**
Prithvi	6	Aakash	30
Apas	12	Vayu	24
Agni	18	Agni	18
Vayu	24	Apas	12
Aakash	30	Prithvi	6

Thursday			
One cycle of 3 hours			
Arohi 1½ hrs		Avrohi 1½ hours	
Bhuta	**min**	**Bhuta**	**Time**
Aakash	30	Vayu	24
Prithvi	6	Agni	18
Apas	12	Apas	12
Agni	18	Prithvi	12
Vayu	24	Aakash	30

Friday			
One cycle of 3 hours			
Arohi 1½ hrs		Avrohi 1½ hours	
Bhuta	**min**	**Bhuta**	**Time**
Apas	12	Prithvi	6
Agni	18	Aakash	30
Vayu	24	Vayu	24
Aakash	30	Agni	18
Prithvi	6	Apas	12

Saturday			
One cycle of 3 hours			
Arohi 1½ hrs		Avrohi 1½ hours	
Bhuta	**min**	**Bhuta**	**Time**
Vayu	24	Agni	18
Aakash	30	Apas	12
Prithvi	6	Prithvi	6
Apas	12	Aakash	30
Agni	18	Vayu	24

times could indicate the difference between male or female. This is not always easy to calculate as females often have strong male qualities and vice versa. I have found that the arohi bhuta usually shows a more active outgoing person whereas the avrohi bhuta shows a calmer, more introverted personality.

The spiritual tendency of an individual can also be dependent on whether the bhuta is rising or falling. A rising bhuta usually indicates an aspiration towards the spiritual while a falling bhuta may show more material desires. This may not always be a clear picture as the sub-bhuta can affect the main bhuta influence.

Identifying your own Bhuta

The first bhuta to rise is the bhuta of the lord of the day. The lord of Tuesday is Mars and his bhuta is agni. On Tuesday the first bhuta arohi (rising) will be agni for 18 minutes, followed by vayu for 24 minutes, aakash for 30 minutes, prithvi for 6 minutes and apas for 12 minutes. Then the avarohi (falling) cycle begins with apas for 12 minutes, prithvi for 6 minutes, aakash for 30 minutes, vayu for 24 minutes and finally agni for 18 minutes. This cycle will continue upward and downward throughout the day and night till the next Sun cycle when the bhuta configuration changes according to its dina lord.

Within each main bhuta there is a smaller cycle of rising and falling bhutas. For example within the 6 minutes of agni, all the five elements will rise and fall. Each person will have a main bhuta and a sub-bhuta according to the birth time. One can make finer divisions as well; up to five bhuta divisions similar to the mahadasha and its sub-dasha cycles.

Arnold Schwarzenegger, Hollywood actor and California's Governor was born on 30 July 1947 at Styer, Austria, 4.10am. It was a Tuesday (this is after midnight but the vedic day will still be Tuesday till sunrise the next day). The sunrise on Tuesday was 5.30am. The first bhuta to rise would be agni.

Seven three-hour cycles would have passed till 2.30am. The arohi portion would add another 1½ hours to 4am. Then ten minutes of the avarohi portion will have passed. The first bhuta of the avarohi on Tuesday is apas which lasts for 12 minutes. Arnold's main bhuta would be apas, but keeping in mind his personality and practical nature, I feel he should have prithvi bhuta. Also his ascendant ruler is Gemini whose ruler Mercury also has a prithvi bhuta and this re-enforces the ascendant. Prithvi has more male energy and Arnold has never shown his softer side, which would have been more evident with an apas bhuta. Therefore I feel that Arnold Schwazenegger may be born slightly later at 4.13am instead of 4.10am.

Dina Nakshatras

Different times of day are ruled by different nakshatras. These nakshatras are not connected to the Moon, they are approximate 48-minute divisions with the exact time depending on the length of the day and night. These are usually used in muhurta where the quality of the nakshatra (malefic or benefic) indicates the quality of time for the auspicious deed. The deity of the dina nakshatra plays a very important part. In the natal chart these nakshatras and their deities have a noticeable influence on energy patterns and modify the results of the dina lord.

In dina nakshatras, Abhijit, the 28th nakshatra is also used. Abhijit means complete victory and is a very auspicious nakshatra where the individual can win over all odds and succeed in life. The daily Abhijit nakshatra happens at the middle of the day exactly at the midheaven and is very powerful.

To calculate the dina nakshatras, divide the day (sunrise to sunset) into 15 equal parts and the night (sunset to sunrise) into 15 equal parts. Each portion of the day is ruled by a nakshatra and is known as a nakshatra muhurta as well. Ardra and Rohini rule two sections of the dina nakshatras each while the others, including Abhijit, rule one each.

More information is given in Chapter 4. It would also be a good idea to study the nakshatra chapter in *The Essentials of Vedic Astrology* to read about the nakshatras and their deities.

Dina Nakshatra Deities

The deities of each dina nakshatra give clues to the nature of the person and also the deity quality they would embody. As dina is about energy, they should try to use the positive aspects of their deities, although sometimes they can get involved with the more negative ones.

Dina Nakshatra Deities

No.	Day	Deity	Night	Deity
1	Ardra	Rudra	Ardra	Rudra
2	Ashlesha	Sarpa	Purva Bhadra	Aja Ekapada
3	Anuradha	Mitra	Uttara Bhadra	Ahirbudhnya
4	Magha	Pitris	Revati	Pushan
5	Dhanishta	Vasus	Ashwini	Ashwini Kumar
6	Purva Ashadha	Apas	Bharani	Yama
7	Uttara Ashadha	Vishwadeva	Krittika	Agni
8	Abhijit	Vidhata, Hari	Rohini	Brahma
9	Rohini	Brahma	Mrigasira	Soma
10	Jyeshta	Indra	Punarvasu	Aditi
11	Vishakha	Indra, Agni	Pushya	Brihaspati
12	Mula	Niritti	Shravana	Vishnu
13	Shatabhishak	Varuna	Hasta	Savitur
14	Uttara Phalguni	Aryaman	Chitra	Twatshar
15	Purva Phalguni	Bhaga	Swati	Vayu

Abhijit – The deity is Vidhata who is the eighth son of Aditi and is another solar god. Vidhata is another name for Brahma, the god who writes the destiny of all new born. Those born during Abhijit have the capacity to write their own destiny and can be so strong that they can also guide others. They need to be careful they don't become too confident.

Ashwini – The ruling deities are Ashwini Kumara, the twin sons of the Sun- god. Ashwini Kumaras are physicians to the gods, very beneficent with great curative powers. They are luminous in nature and had the ability to restore youthfulness and rejuvenate the old. They represent the duality in life by being the connection between heaven and earth, day and night, past and future. Ashwini Kumaras have special healing energies and the ability to rejuvenate.

Bharani – The ruling deity is Yama, the god of death who represents dharma or righteous behaviour. Dharma has four padas or feet which signify truth, purity, penance and charity. They also stand for the gunas (qualities), dravya (sustenance), kriya (action) and jati (caste, creed, genus). Without dharma both gods and demons behave badly. Dharma is a good way of living and means following the right path. Bharani people have to be conscious to follow the right path and need to practice discipline and control.

Krittika – The ruling deity is Agni, the sacred fire, and represents the fire of the mind, the flames of aspiration, the blaze of intellect. Agni symbolises the seven flames, which allow the seven levels of consciousness to operate. The Krittika agni is pure and there is no residual left here. Agni is the messenger of gods and if understood properly gives skill to connect to the higher forces. But agni is also hungry for experience and can get out of control if an individual is only concerned with fulfilling their desires. Then the fire gets bigger and bigger as it gobbles up all it is fed and still wants more. Agni then remains forever thirsty for material experiences and can lose its higher connections.

Rohini – The ruling deity is Brahma. Brahma is the creator of the universe and is one of the main vedic gods. Brahma represents infinity and as individuals we are supposed to be part of Brahma – connected to the universal soul. The Rohini link with Brahma indicates the desire for merging with the absolute, the need to connect the living soul with the eternal, and also shows the need for the individual to be creative. Taurus is a practical impulse and therefore so is Rohini, and the living can only express this yearning for the absolute in a practical way, through passions in real life and by creating new life and relationships. This takes Rohini away from the infinite and further into the world of matter.

Mrigasira – Mrigasira's ruling deity is Soma, which is another name for the Moon. Soma is also a mystical intoxicating nectar that enhances and expands the mind and its faculties. There is a passion for learning here with a multi-talented interest in many things. Soma protects, but is restless and can create problems for itself though its relationships.

Ardra – Rudra, the god of destruction is the presiding deity. Rudra is a form of Shiva, whose mission is to destroy ignorance and direct consciousness towards finding answers and knowledge for ourselves about this incarnation. At Ardra we start to study or learn about the law of nature. The first time we become dissatisfied with the nature of our lives we begin expanding towards differing horizons. The principle of Ardra can be said to destroy what we create, so be careful. Read about Rudra in Chapter 5, chaturdashi tithi.

Punarvasu – The ruling deity is Aditi who is both the female principle and the representation of infinity. Aditi is the mother goddess of the vedas and the mother of Adityas or the Sun gods. She is identified with both Heaven and Earth; hence infinity. Aditi is also the fertility goddess who represents life, creativity and sustenance. Her images are virtually always prone, laying at or below floor level in her characteristic *uttanapad* posture, as though rising from the earth itself, a manifestation of the primordial yoni (vagina) from which all life springs. There are many possible ways of using this energy, both productively and spiritually. These people need to sustain others.

Pushya – The presiding deity is Brihaspati, which is another name for Jupiter. Brihaspati is the primary priest in the Vedas who teaches wisdom and love of truth, and who works for the good of humanity. Brihaspati advised the gods on their religious duties and the purification rituals that are needed for a sattvic life and he is considered the founder of the vedic religion. This dina nakshatra shows the energy used wisely, to help others lead a better life.

Ashlesha – The presiding deity of Ashlesha is Nagas. Nagas are snakes who have great occult powers. The snake carries its poison in a pouch, its body is not filled with poison and it will only use this deadly venom when forced to do so. The poison can be used for healing or for killing and the Nagas have the capacity for both good and bad. Ashlesha can lead people to knowledge, wisdom, wealth and prosperity but it can also take them down the path of danger, self destruction, sexual adventure and unexpected happenings.

Magha – The ruling deity is Pitris, who are the forefathers of humanity with a mission to guide their children on to the right course of life. Pitris, as the deity for Magha, makes the sign very special and the fathers will only interfere if you deviate from the correct path or if you need to ask for inner advice. A greater power will guide at difficult times of life when the going gets tough. Pitris need to be kept happy during shraddha, which occurs annually when the Sun moves through Virgo, during the krishna paksha. This is the time to remember the forefathers and say prayers and feed people in their memory.

Purva Phalguni – The ruling deity Bhaga is the god of good fortune and luck and indicates that the fruits promised by Purva Phalguni are usually highly auspicious. The Indian belief is that good luck shines on you because of the actions in your past life. Bhaga is a Sun god, one of the twelve sons of Aditi, the universal mother. Bhaga also symbolises a woman's womb and procreation, as it is considered a woman's good luck if she bears children. Naturally, Purva Phalguni is the nakshatra where children or creativity is very pronounced.

Uttara Phalguni – Aryaman is another solar god who is the son of Aditi, the universal mother. He is famous for his leadership and the quality of insight, the ability to see beyond the practical realities of life. But he also wants to live this life in the right way and as a nakshatra this bestows those insightful qualities on an incarnating soul while allowing it to recognise that ambitions are limited by the vastness of the task ahead. Aryaman makes the individual very concerned about living life in the right way and with an involvement in social laws.

Hasta – The ruling deity of Hasta is Savitar, one of the twelve sons of Aditi. The twelve sons of Aditi are a symbolic way of saying the twelve signs of the zodiac – Aries to Pisces. Aditi represents infinity and her twelve sons, the zodiac signs, are different expressions of this eternal energy. Savitar is connected to yoga. The practice of yoga allows us to control the mind and body and begin to recognise our inner light. Savitar is also associated with the gayatri mantra, the most important chant connected to the Vedas. Savitar represents the power of sacred words which can cleanse the subtle worlds.

Chitra – The ruling deity is Tvashtar, the celestial architect, whose responsibility is to fashion the outer persona of the individual. Symbolically Tvashtar takes an uncut stone and makes it into a beautiful statue. The uncut stone is the human being encased in the world of matter, their true beauty hidden – Chitra bound in tamas. Tvashtar begins to cut away at the life of matter, a process extremely painful for Chitra. They feel torn apart but slowly their inner light comes through. Tvatshar, the divine artisan, the ideal artist, is also a name for Brahma Prajapati, and for Vishwakarma, the celestial architect who wields the great axe and forged the thunderbolt of Indra. He is vivified and endowed of long life and bestows offspring and generative power. He created Brahmanspati (Jupiter), generated fire along with Heaven and Earth, and created the waters and the Bhrigus who were the ancestors of Venus.

Swati – The ruling deity is Vayu (atmosphere) who rules the material world along with Agni (fire) and Surya (the Sun). Vayu controls the intellect and is linked to Kubera, the god of wealth.

Vayu is the prana – the breath or life force within humans that connects them to the eternal energy. Pranayama or the control of prana forms the basis of yoga. When an individual learns to harness the life force within them, they are able to control life. The yogis believe that we live a certain number of breaths, not a number of years, and the mastery of this breath gives the ability to control the duration of life. Prana disciplines the mind; the practice of pranayama gives the ability to control the wavering mind. Read about vayu in Tithi Chapter 5.

Vishakha – This is the only nakshatra having two deities: Agni and Indra. Agni is the sacred fire, representing the fire of the mind, the flames of aspiration and the blaze of intellect. Agni is also the kundalini, our latent fire. Indra enjoys sensual enjoyment and luxury, but he also destroyed the demon and the destruction of inner demons allows the spiritual energies to flow unhindered. Vishakha is at a junction of life where Agni burns away dross on one side and Indra gives the capability to change the course of life on the other. Vishakha represents both the ascetic and the spiritual within us. The fire of desire – the more you feed the greater it becomes – versus the spiritual fire that burns up old karma and allows you to expose the soul.

Anuradha – Mitra, the ruling deity of Anuradha, is a personification of the Sun. Mitra is one of the twelve sons of Aditi, the universal mother. Mitra means friends, which unites opposites, and Mitra rules daylight. It unveils the experiences of the night, the time an individual spends in harnessing their power. In Anuradha, Mitra exposes the latent potential that has become hidden by a life engulfed in materialism and helps get rid of our darkness by giving us light.

Jyeshta – Indra, the ruling deity of Jyeshta, is considered the god of gods. Indra has the power to control our senses or 'indirayas', a power achieved after hard toils, penance and difficult lessons. Indra can enjoy the sensualities and pleasures of life as he is privy to the secret of how to master them.

Indra was cursed by the guru Gautama for having an affair with his wife Ahilya and his body was pasted with 1000 vaginas. Indra, the gods of gods, also overstepped his mark and therefore had to do tapas for 1000 years before this curse could be modified into a thousand eyes. Jyeshta people feel very powerful; they think they can control themselves and that different rules apply to them, and this arrogance makes them generate their own bad luck, their own demons. It creates baggage throughout their life until they make amends for their transgressions and turn towards a more spiritual journey. Jyeshta learns to control the senses through the practice of yoga and this unites the spiritual with the tangible. Indra is considered one of the gods of yoga as well.

Mula – The ruling deity is Niritti, the goddess of death and destruction. She personifies the destruction of the material sheaths and the laying of foundations on which the spiritual enfoldment can be undertaken. This is the nakshatra of initiation towards spiritual realisation. The destructive nature of Nirriti means that Mula can be self-destructive and spoil things for themselves. They need to remember the importance of roots, tradition and security. Their lives need pruning so that the spiritual tree is ready for new growth, but if they cut down the tree completely their spirituality may die and take a long time to recover.

Purva Ashadha – The ruling deity Apas, the god of water, indicates the transforming nature of this nakshatra. Water is always used in rituals to cleanse and rejuvenate the inner soul. Water is purity and sattvic. Ganga Jal, or the water of the river Ganges, is used at all auspicious occasions. Apas differs from Varuna, the god of the oceans, as Apas is water in a container, spirituality caught in the world of materialism. (Varuna is free flowing). Apas water is pure in essence but can get polluted easily. At Purva Ashadha, the soul wants to cleanse its past sins to prepare for the final journey towards moksha, understanding the purpose of life and being fulfilled.

Uttara Ashadha – The ruling deities, Vishwadeva, are a group of ten universal gods who control the brain cells. They support Uttara Ashadha in reconciling one's past with the journey into the future, and to nurture inner spirituality and talents. Although the Vishwadeva promote social interaction, Uttara Ashadha is not social by nature but it will be so as part of its spiritual responsibility. These people will usually be materially well off but wealth does not give them pleasure. The real joy of Uttara Ashadha comes from finding their true vocation and working towards their higher self.

Shravana – The ruling deity Vishnu is the personification of all the twelve sun gods and therefore represents the entire zodiac. Vishnu means 'he who crosses heights' and he encourages his followers to transverse heights beyond their previous capabilities. Vishnu is the light beyond our perception and will preserve new found spirituality and create the right conditions for developing higher knowledge. He gives Shravana the ability to go beyond a present view of the worlds, and to see the incarnation in a new way. Not many people are willing to perceive their life from a new point of view and are usually afraid of what they will find. When and if they are ready, Vishnu will guide them, nurture their spirituality and give them courage to explore this brave new world.

Dhanishta – The ruling deities are the eight Vasus who are personifications of the Sun: Apas, Dhruva, Soma, Dhara, Anila, Anala, Pratyusha and Prabhas. These deities appear at different stages of manifestation to guide the soul towards its true direction. They are guiding Dhanishta to finish its earthly journey towards the divine and transform ideas from life experiences to move towards higher planes of existence. The deities allow the soul to understand the responsibilities of the family, so that it can pay back its karmic debts and be ready to be liberated. In reality many Dhanishta people forget their soul purpose by taking on the responsibilities and just being involved in giving to others. This one way street can become very frustrating for them.

Shatabhishak – The presiding deity Varuna is an ancient vedic god who rules the ocean and directs the Sun and the wind. He is said to have extraordinary powers to heal and rejuvenate through herbs and medicine and can save you from death and destruction. As the god of the oceans he controls the emotions and the mind and so has the ability to bestow wisdom and change the direction of the mind. He rules both the law and the underworld; there are two sides of his nature – a brighter more positive side as well a darker and secretive one.

Purva Bhadra – The ruling deity Aja Ekapada is the one-footed goat. *Aja* means the unborn, *eka* one and *pada* feet. Aja Ekapada is a deity revered by the Vedas. The goat gives milk, lives alone and is silent or full of creativity that has yet to express itself – it cannot articulate its inner desires. A goat may not be necessarily physically attractive, but it reveals its beauty by giving and supporting life. The ugliness of the goat would be the residue karma that holds Purva Bhadra back. Purva Bhadra can feel ugly, not beautiful, because on a subtle level it sees the issues of personal karma clearly and this is not very appealing. It can make these people suffer with image problems in the material world. However if they take the step forward and overcome their fears, they will find ideas generating which can make their world a lot better.

Uttara Bhadra – The ruling deity Ahir Budhnya is linked to Soma (Moon) and is associated with water and darkness. The passivity of darkness is the mysterious source from which all forms of creation have arisen. Ahir Budhnya, the deep ocean snake, represents the merging of consciousness into the deep sea of eternity. A serpent also represents wisdom, and a snake shedding its skin illustrates rebirth and the cycles of life a soul goes through. Water snakes still need to breathe air, they cannot live completely in the water. Similarly Uttara Bhadra cannot live in the world of spirituality alone; it needs to surface sometimes and honour the material world it lives in.

Revati – The ruling deity Pushan is connected to the divisions of the solar year (varsha) into two parts or ayanas. When the Sun enters the nakshatra of Uttara Ashadha (around 15th of January), Pushan rules this auspicious dawn of the new year, where the death and rebirth of the Sun takes place. Revati represents that time of utter stillness that carries within it a promise of light and the beginning of a new dawn. Pushan guides both the living and the dead; he is the guardian of the transition stages of man, helping people reach their right destination without fear or worry. This can be just their direction in material life or the higher direction where the soul transits from one realm to another. Pushan is connected to the semen, again indicating the seed of creation.

Dina Analysis

The dina shows the planet the soul feels most connected with. The hora will give an added influence to the ruler of the dina; the hora is influencing the dina planet, not the other way around. The dina is what you are and hora is how it changes. If they are both similar, they will totally imbibe the quality of the planet.

The dina lord is the soul's energy. Its strength can make these people confident with what they want to do in this life and supply them with the force to complete their spiritual tasks. Its weakness is that the soul can feel insecure, troubled about its purpose and unable to use the energy properly. This is the primary judgement to make, as the strength of the dina lord is vital for the rest of the chart. Lack of strength of the dina lord can create all sorts of problems in the rashi chart as the soul struggles to express itself properly. So fortifying the dina lord is good and this should not be done by wearing the gems of the lord of the day but through puja, donation, mantras and following the higher path of the dina lord.

We will look at the chart of **Arnold Schwarzenegger** to examine the main points of judgement:

Analyse the natal position of the **dina lord** and its connection to the lagna. Arnold Schwarzenegger's dina is Tuesday. The lord of the day is Mars. This fits perfectly as the energy for the sportsman and body builder and then the action hero of Hollywood. He is a pure pitta personality, but Mars being with Rahu and the 8th house can give him an aggravated pitta that surfaces in over-ambition, anger and health problems. His recent operation for heart surgery could be related to the pitta aggravation. His guna is tamas, which shows his practical down to earth personality. It also can make him steady and dependable.

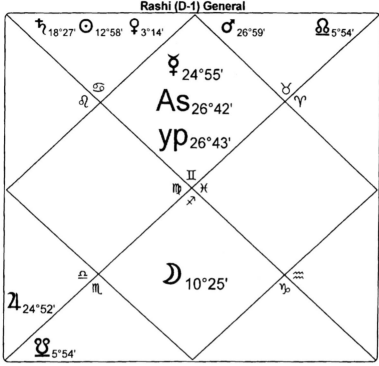

Rashi (D-1) General

Arnold Schwarzenegger
30 July 1947 at Styer, Austria,
4.13am. (Original time was
4.10am but changed to 4.13
using the rising bhuta).
Dina: Tuesday ruled by Mars
Hora: Sun
Rising bhuta: Prithvi
Rising guna: Rajas
Dina nakshatra: Hasta
Sunrise: 05.33
Sunset: 20.45

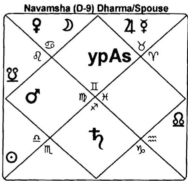

Navamsha (D-9) Dharma/Spouse

What does the dina lord reflect in the rashi chart? If the dina lord is the atmakaraka then the atma's purpose will be best served by allowing the soul to feel in tune with its higher purpose and giving extraordinary strength to fulfil its mission. If the dina lord is the lagna lord, then the soul will give more credence to this incarnation rather than the bigger picture of the atmakaraka. If the dina lord is the Moon lord, then the emotions and intuition dominate. Similarly you can study the other lordship of the dina lord to understand what it is that the soul is reflecting in the natal chart.

In the natal chart Mars is in the 12ᵗʰ house, therefore Arnold would have had to be more famous abroad than at home in Austria. Mars is his atmakaraka, therefore connecting his energy to his soul's purpose. He would have also misused his energy at times. This can create health problems too.

Hora lord will influence according to its relationship with the dina lord. If the hora is atma karaka, then it will influence the soul to follow the soul path but may not be able to change direction. But if the hora is the lagna lord, the lagna will follow the atma and this creates harmony with the purpose of the incarnation. An inimical hora lord can try to take the soul in the wrong direction while a friendly one will help. If the hora and dina lord belong to their conflicting bhuta, there can be problems. If dina is Surya and hora is Venus, their respective bhuta are fire and water. The fire and ambition of the Sun will be dampened by the actions of Venus.

Arnold's Sun is the hora lord. Both Sun and Mars reflect the same bhuta of Agni. Hora lord is compatible with the dina lord.

The rising bhuta. This is the special quality within you, which can influence your prakriti and nature. It also shows whether you express male qualities or female qualities, and which bhuta can easily get out of control and become a dosha. The rising bhuta shows a soul focusing more on the spiritual while the falling bhuta will show an inclination towards materialism.

The rising or falling bhuta should be examined on their own as this will give a clue to the prakriti and the dosha you can most easily be prone to.

Arnold's official time of birth 4.10am gave apas bhuta, which is female and more feminine by quality. If we change this to 4.13am, the rising bhuta would be prithvi. This in my view is a more suitable time of birth. The prithvi ruler is Mercury, which for Arnold Schwarzenegger is the lagna lord and is in Bhadra Mahapurusha yoga in the lagna. The practical aspect of prithvi supports all the fire of the dina and hora lords and gives him a strong constitution.

The rising guna. He is born in the last 1½ hours before sunrise in the rajovela, the time of rajas. He is active, ambitious, seeking answers in the outer world and always on the go.

Dina nakshatra is analysed to see further modifications. The nakshatra always shows the mental make up. See if any planet is placed in the dina nakshatra and study how the nakshatra ruler is placed in the natal chart. The deity of the dina nakshatra protects your energy. If your dina nakshatra is Ashwini, the position of Ketu in the natal chart will give extra information. Also Ashwini Kumaras are the cosmic physicians and therefore this would give an interest in healing and medicine. You can further study all aspects of Ashwini and the other nakshatras from *The Essentials of Vedic Astrology*.

Dina nakshatra is Hasta, connected with taking destiny in your own hands. Arnold Schwarzenegger has changed his life and destiny many times and is a self-made person. Hasta's deity is Savitar, the Sun god, and Arnold Schwarzenegger is a modern day Sun god. A great sportsman turned actor and now a politician and governor of California. He has admirers and a following in each of his three careers. Hasta people feel that they hold their fate in their own hands so make an effort to achieve their ambitions. His roles also show him as the self-sufficient strong hero. Moon, the ruler of Hasta, is well placed in the 7th house and shows support from relationships.

4

The Nakshatras

Nakshatra literally means a star in Sanskrit. A star is a point of cosmic light. To study the Moon's movement across the backdrop of the stars gave early civilizations an understanding of the deeper meaning of life. One nakshatra is the distance the moon travels through the background of the stars in one day.

Although in natal astrology we would study the positions of all the planets in their nakshatras, in panchanga we are only concerned with the Moon's position. This is known as janma nakshatra. The Moon is the significator of the mind and therefore each nakshatra's prime connection is with the ebb and flow of the mind. As dina reflects the soul, nakshatra reflects the mind, and this is the second most important component of the panchanga.

A day is divided into four portions, sunrise, midday, sunset and midnight, and the nakshatras are also divided into four parts known as padas. These four parts also reflect the four cardinal directions and the four main aims of the incarnating soul. The padas link the divine part of the Moon's energy to that of the Sun. The nakshatras and the rashis are joined together by the navamsha and the padas.

The Panchamahabhuta is Vayu
The bhuta of the nakshatras is vayu. The Moon placed in the nakshatras reflects the wavering of the mind, forever moving, active, and agitated if not properly utilised. Like the mind, vayu is not easy to control, and to further complicate matters each nakshatra has its own bhuta that additionally aggravates or calms the vayu. The restless Moon travels from one nakshatra to another seeking the meaning of life, trying to unravel the karma of the past and find suitable answers in the present. Vayu's planetary ruler is Saturn.

The Chakra is Anahata
Vayu rules anahata or the heart chakra. The nakshatra at birth will indicate how we deal with the chakras. If one is born in a difficult nakshatra (Bharani, Ardra, Mula etc.), or the Moon is in a hard

conjunction or weak, we can feel our heart chakra being blocked. We must study the particular bhuta of the nakshatra as well.

Uses of Panchanga Nakshatra

The reasons for needing to know the Moon nakshatra in panchanga are the following:

1. The quality of the mind. Although The Moon is not analysed philosophically or spiritually in the panchanga; that is left to chart analysis. I feel this is the most important aspect of the nakshatras as they show the true mind of an individual through the Moon's position.

2. The position of the Moon in a nakshatra decides the start of the vimshottari dasha. The lord of the nakshatra is the lord of the first dasha. This dasha reveals the total karmic pattern of the life of the individual.

3. Nama nakshatra – the name given at birth – is decided from the alphabet belonging to the specific pada that the individual is born under. *Nama* means name and the importance of getting the name from the birth nakshatra is that the name becomes a mantra, calming the vayu of the nakshatra each time it is spoken.

4. The bhuta of the nakshatra decides which of the panchamahabhuta are controlling the quality of the mind and the chakras.

5. From the janma nakshatra certain nakshatras have special significance. They are known as *nadi nakshatras*. There are nine nadi nakshatras in all: six nadi nakshatras for everyone and three additional ones for nations and their leaders.

6. There are some nakshatras like Bharani, Krittika, Jyeshta and Mula that bring issues with them. Also birth in Gandanta nakshatra is a very karmic condition and could make for a troubled life unless properly understood.

7. If your nakshatra is the same as your parents', then certain remedies are prescribed by Parashara for removing the negativity. (More in Remedial Measures, Chapter 8).

8. The birth nakshatra is used in all prayers. In yagyas, or in temples, the priests ask for the janma nakshatra so that they can propitiate the deities correctly. Subtly this helps the vayu to calm down and remain like a gentle breeze rather than a destructive hurricane.

First Vimshottari Dasha

Depending on the placement of the Moon the first vimshottari dasha is revealed and accordingly the whole pattern of life. Saturn, Rahu or Ketu as the first dashas are usually difficult ones to have, although it is dependent on the natal ascendant whether the first dasha ruler is a good planet for you personally. The dashas show how the chart reveals itself and the dasha pattern decides the positive or negative times of life, the expression of prarabhdha karma, or the tests of past karma to be met in this life. It can be considered a map of destiny but it is not completely fixed. We always have choices in the form of kriyamana karma (free will) on how we will react to the karmic patterns revealed by the nakshatras and the first dasha.

Nakshatra	First Vimshottari Dasha
Ashwini	Ketu
Bharani	Venus
Krittika	Sun
Rohini	Moon
Mrigasira	Mars
Ardra	Rahu
Punarvasu	Jupiter
Pushya	Saturn
Ashlesha	Mercury
Magha	Ketu
Purva Phalguni	Venus
Uttara Phalguni	Sun
Hasta	Moon
Chitra	Mars
Swati	Rahu
Vishakha	Jupiter
Anuradha	Saturn
Jyeshta	Mercury
Mula	Ketu
Purva Ashadha	Venus
Uttara Ashadha	Sun
Shravana	Moon
Dhanishta	Mars
Shatabhishak	Rahu

Purva Bhadra	Jupiter
Uttara Bhadra	Saturn
Revati	Mercury

Nama Nakshatra

According to vedic tradition, the first letter of your birth name was chosen from the special consonant or vowel related to your birth nakshatra. This way you are perpetually connected to your birth energy. The name becomes like a mantra and whenever someone says your name it creates an auspicious energy.

The nakshatras reflect the complete *akshara* (alphabet) of Sanskrit. Each nakshatra has four special consonants or vowels, one for each pada. The moment a child is born the parents ask the jyotishi or priest for the right consonant/vowel to name their child correctly. This is known as nama nakshatra. The choice is not from any four consonants of the Moon nakshatra but the one that belongs to the specific pada the Moon was in. This is a tradition that has got lost as many don't know the significance of the nama nakshatra. It can be difficult to find Sanskrit alphabet names that convert into western names but there are many that do match. If you want to give yourself a vedic name you should chose one compatible to your birth Moon. You can also check the nakshatra and pada of your given name and see how you resonate with this nakshatra. There is a technique which uses the nama nakshatra to construct a completely new chart and is used especially for those who do not know their birth date/ time. The nama nakshatra is also used in prashna. The consonants for the nakshatras are given below.

Nama Nakshatra Table: Special consonants/vowels for nakshatras

	Nakshatra	Pada			
		1	2	3	4
1.	Ashwini	Chu	Chey	Cho	La
2.	Bharani	Li	Lu	Ley	Lo
3.	Krittika	Aa	Ee	U	A
4.	Rohini	O	Va	Vee	Vo
5.	Mrigasira	Vay	Vo	Ka	Kee

6.	Ardra	Koo	Ghaa	Jna	Chcha
7.	Punarvasu	Kay	Ko	Ha	Hee
8.	Pushya	Hoo	Hay	Ho	Daa
9.	Ashlesha	Dee	Doo	Day	Do
10.	Magha	Maa	Mee	Moo	May
11.	Purva Phalguni	Mo	Taa	Tee	Too
12.	Uttara Phalguni	Tay	To	Paa	Pee
13.	Hasta	Pu	Shaa	Na	Thaa
14.	Chitra	Pay	Po	Raa	Re
15.	Swati	Ru	Ray	Pa	Ta
16.	Vishakha	Thee	Thuu	Thay	Thou
17.	Anuradha	Naa	Nee	Nou	Nay
18.	Jyeshta	No	Ya	Yee	You
19.	Mula	Yay	Yo	Baa	Bee
20.	Purva Ashadha	Bu	Dha	Bha	Dha
21.	Uttara Ashadha	Bay	Bo	Jaa	Jee
22.	Shravana	Ju	Jay	Jo	Gha
23.	Dhanishta	Gaa	Gee	Goo	Gay
24.	Shatabhishak	Go	Sa	See	Sou
25.	Purva Bhadra	Say	So	Daa	Dee
26.	Uttara Bhadra	Du	Tha	Aa	Jna
27.	Revati	De	Do	Chaa	Chee

Tiger Woods'[1] nakshatra is Jyeshta – pada 4. The name would begin with *You* and in common with most people he is not named according to the nakshatra.

There is another technique in understanding how the nama nakshatra can be studied. Which nakshatra does the first akshara of the name fall into? As the name is like a mantra and said thousands of times, its sound vibrations have a great impact. When analysing someone's name, you must use the name they are popularly known by. Tiger Woods was given the birth name Eldrick, but he is popularly known as Tiger. His name therefore begins with Ti – which would resonate with the 'Tee' of Purva Phalguni in Leo. The next step is to see what house the name falls into, and for such a successful personality as Tiger Woods his

---

1.   Tiger Woods: 30 Dec 1975, 22.50 PST, Long Beach, CA, USA.

name should fall in the kendra (1,4,7,10) or trikona (5,9) houses, re-enforcing his personality. If it fell in dushthana houses (6,8,12), it would indicate a struggle. Tiger Woods' official birth time of 22.50 gives a Virgo ascendant, putting his name nakshatra into the twelfth house, but if you rectify his birth time to 22.45 it gives him a Leo lagna, which seems more appropriate for Tiger Woods anyway. His nama nakshatra would fall into the lagna and whenever his name was said it would resound with his lagna and give him the extra sound vibrations.

It is not essential to change your name to the nama nakshatra if your name already falls in a good house in the rashi. Moreover if the Moon is weak or placed in a negative house, having the name according to the nama nakshatra may weaken the chart as it promotes the quality of the Moon.

For those who do not know their time of birth the technique of using the nama nakshatra as an ascendant is very useful. Check which akshara your given name represents then make that degree your ascendant and read the chart from there. If your name is Margaret, the nama nakshatra would fall in the first pada of Magha which is between 0°00 to 3°20 Leo. If the birthday is on 25 July 1975 in London, time unknown, you would take the ascendant to be 0°00 to 3°20 Leo, which gives a time between 7.24am to 7.43am. This gives amazing results and can be further rectified to make the time more precise. If you check this technique with someone whose data you know, you will find that the nama nakshatra reveals a lot. Dashas and transits can also be read from this chart.

Nakshatra Bhuta

While the bhuta of the nakshatras is vayu, each nakshatra has its own bhuta which modifies the overall bhuta. The Moon is usually nervous, stressed and fickle by nature as it is always travelling. The same can be said of the mind. We need to work on the mind, to calm it down and not allow mental stresses to increase. Some nakshatras find it easier to deal with this than others. The vayu nakshatras Jyeshta, Mula, Purva Ashadha, Uttara Ashadha and Shravana, are the most vulnerable to the forces of stress; prone to worry and mental unease. The main aspect of vayu should be remembered: if the mind concentrates on being productive it can get rid of negative thinking and the stresses that come with it.

Bhuta	Nakshatra
Prithvi	Ashwini
	Bharani
	Krittika
	Rohini
	Mrigasira
Apas	Ardra
	Punarvasu
	Pushya
	Ashlesha
	Magha
	Purva Phalguni
Agni	Uttara Phalguni
	Hasta
	Chitra
	Swati
	Vishakha
	Anuradha
Vayu	Jyeshta
	Mula
	Purva Ashadha
	Uttara Ashadha
	Shravana
Aakash	Dhanishta
	Shatabhishak
	Purva Bhadra
	Uttara Bhadra
	Revati

Nadi Nakshatras

Nadi means a pulse and these nakshatras offer secret clues about themselves. The nadi nakshatras highlight areas of life like career and subtle mind, and certain nakshatras from the position of the birth nakshatra can be extremely negative for the individual. Transits to these nadi nakshatras are significant and can create issues according to their nature. Also contact with people who reflect your nadi nakshatras can be either very good or extremely difficult. The list follows on the next page.

1. **Janma nakshatra** – is the 1ˢᵗ nakshatra, the same as at birth. When it returns to this position it is not a good time to do auspicious deeds. If children are born with the same janma nakshatra as their father, brother, mother or sister, it is not considered good and a remedial measure is advised by Parashara.

2. **Karma nakshatra** – is the 10ᵗʰ nakshatra from janma and indicates the profession or what work the individual will do. This is the next nakshatra ruled by the same lord as the janma. If the janma is Ashlesha, then the karma nakshatra will be the next nakshatra ruled by Mercury, which is Jyeshta.

3. **Sanghatika nakshatra** – is the 16ᵗʰ nakshatra from janma. *Sangha* means unions, groups, associations and close or intimate relationships. *Tika* means to challenge, to hurt, wound or injure. Sanghatika means close associations that are challenging and have the ability to hurt and injure. This is a difficult nakshatra, and when malefic planets transit here, they would create problems. Relationships with someone representing the 16ᵗʰ nakshatra from your janma Moon nakshatra usually create challenging situations in relationships and can be destructive. If the janma is Krittika then sanghatika nakshatra will be Jyeshta. There is incompatibility between Krittika and Jyeshta Moons as Jyeshta has the ability to hurt or challenge Krittika. They may form intimate relationships with each other but these may not be productive for Krittika.

4. **Samudaya nakshatra** – is the 18ᵗʰ nakshatra from janma and is an auspicious one. Its name means ascent, rising, war, battle, auspicious moment, and events taking place in this nakshatra are regarded as positive.

5. **Vinasha nakshatra** – is the 23ʳᵈ from janma and means ruin, annihilation and destruction. Starting anything good in a vinasha nakshatra is not beneficial. Be careful of the transits of Saturn, Mars or Rahu; even the benefics in this nakshatra may not be able to give good results. To start a new project when the Moon is in this nakshatra is not advisable and you may find relationships with individuals having this nakshatra are not always happy or profitable.

6.   **Manasa nakshatra** – is the 25th from janma. *Manas* means the mind and this nakshatra gives a deeper understanding and further clues as to how the mind works.

The three added nakshatras are:

1.   Nakshatra of the caste – caste is just a classification of types of jobs. In Shloka 43, in the Nakshatras Chapter of the classic book *Muhurta Chintamani*[2], seven castes prevalent in those times are listed, but it adds that things may be different now. So we should reclassify nakshatras according to our own times and take these nakshatras not to represent you, the individual, but a section of society. Good transits will help the community while negative ones create problems. When difficult planets transit these nakshatras, that section of society and their leaders could suffer. If Saturn is in Jyeshta by transit for example, it would affect the working classes and their leaders. (In the UK a leader of the Labour Party could be termed a working class leader). Ketu's transit of Magha would affect farmers, and so on. We should study where the most difficult transits are taking place as that is the area of the community that would be affected. The list of the nakshatra castes given in *Muhurta Chintamani* is:

Caste	Nakshatras
Brahmins (priests)	Purva Phalguni, Purvashadha, Purva Bhadra, Krittika
Kshatriya (warriors and establishment)	Uttara Phalguni, Uttarashadha, Uttara Bhadra and Pushya
Farmers	Revati, Anuradha, Magha and Rohini
Vaishya (businessmen)	Punarvasu, Hasta, Abhijit and Ashwini
Criminals	Mula, Ardra, Swati, Shatabhishak
Shudra (workers)	Mrigasira, Jyeshta, Chitra, Dhanishta
Chandala (outcasts, immigrants)	Ashlesha, Vishakha, Shravana, Bharani

2.   *Muhurtha Chintamani*, translated by GC Sharma, Sagar Publication, 1996.

2.   Nakshatra of the country/ company/ organisation – this is the Moon nakshatra of the birth of the country. India's nakshatra for its independence on 15 August 1947 is Pushya. At the birth of the United Kingdom, 1 January 1801, the janma nakshatra was Punarvasu. At the birth of the United States of America (Jim Kelleher chart), 4 July 1776, it was Shatabhishak. For countries this shows the mind of its people, how they think and feel. Transits to this nakshatra will create positive or negative issues for the country.

3.   Nakshatra of the abhisheka – the time of the coronation. In the case of election charts of presidents and prime ministers, this is the time they take office, not when they are elected. Abhisheka nakshatra can also be used for anyone powerful taking office and its quality affects those who work below them. Transits to this nakshatra may be positive or negative according to their quality.

Nakshatra Gandanta, the Spiritual Knot

Gand means a knot, *anta* means the end, so Gandanta is the knot at the end. A well-tied knot is one that is very difficult to unravel, and the more you try to untie it the tighter it becomes. Gandanta represents a knot within ourselves, a deep issue to which we are trying to become reconciled. Gandanta describes the junction points in the zodiac where the solar and lunar zodiac meet and these are particularly connected with times of soul growth. These points are at the junctions of Pisces (Revati) and Aries (Ashwini), Cancer (Ashlesha) and Leo (Magha), Scorpio (Jyeshta) and Sagittarius (Mula). The nakshatra Gandanta is when the Moon is situated within 48 minutes either side of these points. For panchanga, being born at nakshatra Gandanta is considered very tough and remedial measures are given for this birth.

When the Moon is placed in these powerfully karmic degrees it shows uncertainty as we try to unravel the secret knot that will take us to the next level. There would be an immediate change of dasha from Mercury to Ketu after birth if the Moon is placed at the end degrees of a sign/nakshatra or the start of life at the beginning of a Ketu dasha if the Moon is placed in the early degrees of the sign.

The Gandanta degrees are usually between water and fire signs. We read in the Panchamahabhuta chapter how water and fire are inimical elements and all planets placed in this junction are adversely affected. In panchanga the main attention is given to the Moon's position.

Degrees	Rashi	Nakshatra
29°12 – 30°00	Pisces	Revati
00°00 – 00°48	Aries	Ashwini
29°12 – 30°00	Cancer	Ashlesha
00°00 – 00°48	Leo	Magha
29°12 – 30°00	Scorpio	Jyeshta
00°00 – 00°48	Sagittarius	Mula

The Moon in the nakshatra Gandanta is particularly powerful as it shows that one is born either at the end of a Mercury dasha or the beginning of Ketu dasha. The end of a Mercury dasha usually reveals a soul reconciling with past karma and there can be many debts to pay. Mercury dashas usually have poisonous endings whereas Ketu represents the past life and the soul is burdened with its karma. The problem is that at this time the individual is only a child and does not have the personal resources to deal with this. Although parents can be affected by this Gandanta, as a child we are unaware of what is happening and its influence stays with us for life. There can be many difficulties to be faced and adjustments to be made as we move from one level of spiritual growth into the next.

The Gandanta
The Pisces/Revati and Aries/Ashwini Gandanta shows the ending of one cycle of soul growth and the beginning of its next stage. This is where the inner self begins its journey of life. If the Moon is in the Pisces portion of the Gandanta, it relates to ending experiences, where the soul has reached its full maturity at the present level of growth and is ready to move to another cycle and a different set of issues. The soul is closing the door to one cycle and it does not end easily, usually there can be inner storms as the soul destroys one way to make way for a new life. In the Aries/Ashwini portion of Gandanta, the soul is connected to the past life but it has begun a new cycle of soul growth. The soul is insecure as it has not yet understood its role in the new incarnation. This creates confusion and brings powerful influences, which are at times difficult to understand for both positions.

The Cancer/Ashlesha and Leo/Magha Gandanta is where the soul ends its search in the world of rajas, where it has been going from place to place to seek answers about its incarnations and the true identity of the eternal soul. This is an outer journey and the result does not bring any answers but it creates an involvement in the world of tamas, the material life. The Cancer/Ashlesha stage is where the outer search must end and it must give up its search to settle down. But it is not ready to do so. The transition from rajas to tamas is never easy; the ruling deity of Ashlesha is Naga, the wise serpents. At this stage there is a shedding of the skin to grow another; an experience which changes the mind and psyche and can be extremely painful, but is necessary for the soul to grow into another dimension. The soul is vulnerable and exposed at the Gandanta point. At the Magha/Leo stage, the soul is finally getting ready to experience life in tamas. It has not as yet grown a new skin. It is idealistic and not fully aware of the rules of materialism. This is a junction point, therefore the intellectual changes already experienced at the Cancer/Ashlesha level are still very strong.

Scorpio/Jyeshta and Sagittarius/Mula Gandanta is the most difficult of the three Gandantas as it moves the inner soul in its final direction towards merging with the universal consciousness. This is the stage where the material ties need to be cut and the soul must realize its true spiritual direction. It is where the maximum churning of inner turmoil takes place. Even when the soul knows this path is towards its true self, it fights against it. This is never an easy task and it creates many psychological or physical blocks that need to be tackled with patience and maturity. At the Scorpio/Jyeshta stage, there is an immense churning of inner emotion, where material sheaths break up and lead to inner change. If there is resistance to change it makes it even more difficult for the person. On a material level this can be tough whereas on a spiritual level it leads towards activating latent spiritual power.

At the Mula/Sagittarius stage, the soul recognizes it has to change and in many ways it already has. But it still remains tied to its past and its earthly needs, which Mula, meaning 'the root', suggests. This root is buried in the ground or in deep material realms. There are two ways open to Mula: one is to cut away completely from its material roots and begin the spiritual journey and the other is to trim the excess of negativity while remaining still rooted in this world. At the Mula stage one has to be very careful not to be self-destructive and destroy what is still valid. The person should treat their life as a precious plant, which needs pruning so that new shoots of spirituality can grow while the dead wood of materialism is cut out. If they cut the roots, their insecurity can lead to the spirituality dying away. Jyeshta has to wean itself away from its desires whereas Mula must avoid destroying all that is precious to them when they are ridding themselves of karmic debris. Usually a Jyeshta Moon has relationship issues whereas Mula brings problems with parents.

There are remedial measures for birth in all the Gandanta Moons given in the Remedial Measures Chapter 8.

Moon in the Nakshatras

Ashwini
00°00 to 13°20 Aries

Aries deals with a new cycle of the soul's journey, *Ashwins* are the harbingers of usha or dawn. Dawn brings with it a very special energy, the promise of a new tomorrow while still attached to the mysterious night. The representation of dawn indicates the link of the soul to the past lives that are going to help fashion the future. Ashwins are the link between the darkness of the night and the brightness of the day and Ashwini expresses this twin energy of dark and light, practical and spiritual, dynamic and calm, idealism and pragmatism. Ashwini illustrates a living soul very much in touch with its roots in the past life and as yet not ready to let it go.

Ashwin means a cavalier or a horse tamer. The symbol of Ashwini is also a horse. Horses represent our senses, our desires and creative energy. A cavalier's ability to ride horses is connected to the ability to master desires, and the Moon in Ashwini is keen to experience all desires. These people usually begin by embracing freedom and experiencing every craving, but they soon realise that fulfilling one desire only creates another and there is no fulfilment. Finally they learn to sacrifice their desires for their greater happiness, and learn to give them up. The concept of sacrifice is imbedded within Ashwini.

The past life planet Ketu rules Ashwini. Ketu aims for self-realisation, a state of absolute perfection where there is perpetual bliss and the soul is released from the cycles of unhappiness and pain. This is the urge of the first dasha of Ketu for Ashwini Moon. Although these people may be too young to appreciate what Ketu brings into their life, this Ketu energy remains with them throughout their years. They search for enlightenment but may settle for the mundane if their desires are overpowering. Ketu has the ability to give up all desires but as the past life planet it can also obscure the true picture of present reality. These people are trying to fulfil what they felt was left unfinished in previous lifetimes and this may create a pattern of behaviour where they yearn for the beautiful past and do not not pay enough attention to the present. The Ashwini Moon can be very dissatisfied. The other facet is that the ability to let go of desires gives ultimate power. These people can be very powerful if they are able to control their spiritual and emotional needs.

Bharani
13°20 to 26°40 Aries
The quality of Aries shifts here. The living soul is considering relationships and within Bharani the sexual desires are strong. *Bharani* means 'cherishing' 'supporting' and 'nourishing'. The symbol for Bharani is yoni, the female reproductive organ. This establishes Bharani as a channel for creation whether by sexual act or incubation of other creative energies.

Bharani people are the sensualists of the zodiac. They are forever searching for their spiritual self but are usually most happy expressing their sensual one. If they allow their sexual energy to become their creative channel, either by having children or through ideas, arts, and music, they can be very strong. Mars gives them an earthiness while Venus creates a love of fine things. Bharani cherishes and supports the soul in the womb till it is ready to be born, and in a wider sense Bharani can be an incubator of ideas and thoughts as it nourishes creativity in any form: arts, ideas, thoughts and soul.

Venus rules this nakshatra, which celebrates female sexuality as the symbol of fertility and fruitfulness. In India certain ancient monuments like Khajurao honour female sexuality in their immense sculptures. They personify fertility, harmony and growth. The Bharani Moon sees sexuality as an expression of divinity, and as Venus is the first dasha, these people develop their sensual nature and love of good things from an early age. The Bharani Moon emphasises the passion and sensuality of Aries but these people do not always know how to control their passions and can make unwise choices in relationships. Yet Bharani gives the strength to control their emotions and passions if they want to. With the Moon in Bharani they can live a life of excess to begin with, then as they learn to control their wayward emotions, develop their higher self. If they misuse their sexuality, or place an over-emphasis on sex and promiscuity, it can deplete their inner resources. There is an ascetic side to their nature as penance requires giving up all pleasures and voluntarily living in isolation and discomfort.

Krittika
26°40 to 30°00 Aries 00°00 to 10°00 Taurus
Krittika straddles two signs, Aries and Taurus. One pada of Krittika is in Aries and the rest are in Taurus . Courage, confidence and power are the key features of Krittika.

Krit means to cut or divide and *tika* means to challenge. These people are never afraid to challenge and cut through opposition as Krittika is a nakshatra considered fierce and destructive. The myth of Krittika is connected to the demon Taraka and the birth of Kartika, the warrior Mars. Taraka received the blessing of Brahma, the creator of the universe, saying that only a seven-day-old son of Shiva could kill him. Shiva was an ascetic who was meditating in the Himalayas and had no intention of producing a son. So the gods manipulated to get the semen of Shiva through Kamadeva, the god of love. When they obtained his seed, the six Krittikas incubated it. From that seed Kartika the warrior god was born and destroyed Taraka when he was seven days old. This myth indicates the immense power of Krittika. The Krittika Moon expresses the pure qualities of Mars: of fighting a righteous war, defending the oppressed and leading the world to a better place.

Krittika Moon people can become healers or warriors. Krittika has the capacity to create powerful people of courage and confidence who are not afraid to confront difficult situations. It is important to remember that Krittika represents the ability to challenge difficulties and oppositions. The control of the mind is strong here because the Moon is exalted in Krittika, yet these people must watch their destructive tendencies. The mind wants to create, but the fire of Krittika can burn everything in sight without taking care of what should or should not be preserved.

The Sun rules Krittika and the Sun signifies authority, power, vitality and strength. Krittika is the true expression of the Sun, Mars and Agni. It is warm, fierce and supportive. This is all about the controlled and wise use of power, the ability to love and be warm rather than show aggressiveness and cruelty – also qualities of Mars and the Sun. The first dasha of the Sun makes the Krittika Moon come face to face with their strengths and weaknesses from a young age.

Rohini
10°00 to 23°20 Taurus

Rohini in Sanskrit means red, which relates to passion and sensuality. Rohini is considered the favourite wife of the Moon. According to the mythology the 27 nakshatras are the 27 wives of Soma, the male Moon god, and Soma stayed with each for one day a month. The other wives, jealous of the Moon's infatuation with Rohini, complained to Prajapati, who cursed the Moon, causing him to lose his power totally and then regain it. This became the waxing and waning lunar cycles. The 27 symbolic wives of the Moon reflect your differing moods and your ability to be involved in more than one relationship at a time.

Rohini is the first realisation of love, possessiveness, passion and ecstasy but it is also the start of making yourself emotionally weak as one person or one spiritual ideology does not satisfy. The lustfulness of Taurus is very strong here; there are huge passions and desires. Rohini's passions and Taurus' lustfulness can find the same voice and infidelity or multiple relationships can be common. Although the search can be for true love, its expression may involve many sexual relationships and the inability to find satisfaction. While Rohini's motivation remains idealistic its expression can sometimes be very earthy and many find it difficult to reconcile the two.

Taurus establishes itself through creativity but within Rohini the mind begins to roam. The Moon is not satisfied by the steadiness of Taurus and at Rohini the Moon is beginning its search. Usually this journey begins when you are totally comfortable with the way life is at present. There is secure feeling that this journey will only bring pleasure and the consequences are not always recognised. The need to explore takes us into new areas of life where the old ways become dated and dissatisfied.

The Moon rules Rohini and the Moon signifies the mind, both emotional and intellectual. The Moon is the physical embodiment of our soul, the ebb and flow of our feelings, and the need for change on a daily basis. Just as the Moon roams the night skies in a perpetual search so the mind remains unsettled in its wandering search for answers. The first dasha is of the Moon and shows that the restlessness of the mind begins at a young age and remains throughout life unless one channels it towards creativity, ideas and differing interests.

Mrigasira
23°20 to 30°00 Taurus and 00°00 to 06°40 Gemini

Mriga means a deer and *sira* means head. In Indian mythology the head of the deer is a representation of the Moon. The lunar energy that is reflected in Mrigasira makes these people restless, sensitive and emotional. Mrigasira essentially shows the beginning of a search in the world of illusion. The deer here is the golden deer that we all search for but can never find.

Mrigasira straddles Taurus and Gemini. One of the important aspects of Mrigasira is the dichotomy of its active/passive nature. These people want to be something yet will not act on it. This aspect becomes very strong in Taurus Mrigasira as Taurus enjoys the comforts of life and Mrigasira will not let the present life be disrupted, even when feeling issues acutely, and they take the easy way out. Gemini Mrigasira also tends to talk about injustices but not take any positive action. The quality of Mrigasira that emerges in Gemini, the thinking nakshatra in the thinking sign, can create great inner conflicts.

Self image is usually a problem for Mrigasira. Their active/passive nature makes them explore many new areas but their reluctance to do much about them leads to frustrations. Mrigasira must learn to use the mind properly and focus on what they want to do. If their life is not right, they must do something about it. Mars, its ruler, was born to defend and Mrigasira can only live in a negative situation for so long. If things become unbearable they will fight their corner and take the right action. Mrigasira can get very angry unless it finds an outlet for Mars by learning to speak out against injustice and not storing everything within.

Mars being the first dasha brings lots of energy at a young age. A Mrigasira mind needs to be occupied from the beginning otherwise it can lead to restlessness, going from one relationship to another, one idea to another. The more security these people seek, the less secure they feel. Mrigasira should learn to use their Mars and explore the new.

Ardra
06°40 to 20°00 Gemini

Ardra means green, moist, or like a teardrop. The moistness of the eyes can blur the picture yet we feel renewed and refreshed after tears have fallen. At the cosmic stage of Ardra you are dissatisfied with your present surroundings and start looking for answers. The ability to be both confused and enlightened at the same time is possible here. The symbol of Ardra is the head, where the brain or the mind is situated. The brain is formed by experiences from past karma. How you react in this life is the sum total of the experiences of those karmas.

The Ardra Moon is connected to intellectual fertility, the ability of the mind to create. Ardra is both enhanced by sharp thinking but limited by intellectual barriers. The limitations of intellect can blur your mind or you can use your intelligence to connect to the subconscious and create fertile grounds for new growth. The ability to be self-destructive is strong in Ardra as dissatisfaction can blur the picture when you feel life is not giving you what you want. If you destroy the present way of living to move forward be careful not to throw out the baby with the bathwater and destroy what is valid and good for you. The Moon is in its enemy sign and a difficult nakshatra with a tempestuous nature and many emotional storms raging within. Despite their lack of clarity these storms can bring new shoots of growth. Learn to recognise your strengths and weaknesses, control the stormy nature, and this can be a good place for mental fertility.

Ardra is ruled by Rahu. Rahu is the projection of past life issues into the present, obsessed with externalising the past through current experiences. As the first dasha Rahu is never easy, delivering a childhood (up to 18 years) struggling with shadows that you are not yet able to face. There can be ups and downs, great ambitions and great disappointments, all coming as part of the package. Even when Rahu is well placed in the chart, as the first dasha it is not easy to handle, leaving some emotional scars that we need to work with in adult life.

Punarvasu
20°00 to 30°00 Gemini, 00°00 to 03°20 Cancer

Punah means again and *vasu* means brilliant like rays of light. Vasu is also the home of the soul and Punarvasu relates to the vasus, the solar deities, that appear at different stages of the soul's birth to guide it towards its true direction. They are like Sun rays that bring divine messages to Earth. Punarvasu is connected to the transmigration of the soul, where the soul lives in different bodies in search for its true home and in doing so transforms ideas from higher planes into earthly life. These people enjoy travel, whether from country to country or on different levels of consciousness. They can change homes many times.

Punarvasu has a special significance for the Moon. It is the beginning cycle in the padas and the navamsha, but more importantly two amshas are vargottama (one in Cancer punarvasu) and one is pushkara. Therefore there is real support for the Moon on this journey. It is the first time the soul searches for a home for itself in the outer world and it needs to to feel comfortable and to be loved to fully explore this new world in all its glory. After the intellectual awareness that Mrigasira and Ardra bring, the mind wants to move to a different realm, even though it may not know all the rules of engagement here. In Punarvasu there is a vulnerability due to lack of experience as well as a courage and confidence to go into new areas. The journey of Punarvasu is extremely well supported and an essential part of the soul's growth. Whatever these people want from life, they are assisted and integrated with the purpose of the soul. It is not always easy to fulfill what the soul demands but the Moon in Punarvasu will make sure you do so.

The search in Gemini Punarvasu is not always in the right way. There are dissatisfactions, too many questions asked and not so much use of instinct. Those who know how to ask the right questions will find this journey inspirational and full of joy. Punarvasu in Cancer does this. There is new vitality, a new home for the soul and the recognition of this new identity – multi-layered, multidimensional, different yet the same.

While Punarvasu Cancer gets the best possible conditions, the main difference between Cancer and Gemini Punarvasu is that in Gemini, Punarvasu thinks analytically and is only looking for answers in the outer world. They see the world around them and recognise this as their new reality, but in Cancer, Punarvasu gets in touch with their soul, with their intuitive self.

Jupiter, the celestial teacher, rules Punarvasu. Wisdom is their inheritance and these people are wise beyond their years even as children. Unless Jupiter is badly afflicted it should give an easy start to life. The first dasha lord, Jupiter, is one of the best to have. The Moon can be unsettled in Punarvasu despite the wisdom of Jupiter as the mind needs to see the world from different perspectives – and this is where the true knowledge comes to Punarvasu.

Pushya
03°20 to 16°40 Cancer

Cancer can seamlessly merge two diverse issues together and it is in Pushya that desires are nurtured and cherished. *Pushya* means to 'nourish' or 'thrive'. Pushya works to nourish others and create perfect conditions so that they can thrive in the material world. This is a pit stop before the true action. The soul sees and learns about its new life but still has a strong connection with the past. The soul's qualities are being harnessed for materialism, which is the expression of the signs Leo to Scorpio ahead.

The symbol of Pushya is a flower; the expression of latent faculties, the outward expression of inner ideas. A flower also blooms for others and may not recognise its own beauty and at Pushya's stage there is a need to work for others, an idealistic sense of being. Saturn controls this important task as Saturn rules Pushya. Saturn is the great teacher of cosmic truths but his influence is tough to deal with, not the easiest to have as your first dasha. As Saturn can control up to nineteen years of the start of life, it usually brings a disciplined childhood where personal needs are not paramount. Clients tell me that the Saturn dasha childhood is not easy, but as they grow older and out of the Saturn dasha they find their lost childhood and youth.

Ashlesha
16°40 to 30°00 Cancer

Ashlesha means to 'embrace' – the soul embracing life so that it can act out its karma. As soon as we embrace life we are subject to the rules and regulations of the Earth. We are involved in the process of life and death, happiness and unhappiness. Ashlesha needs to move from a state of detachment to attachment.

Mercury rules Ashlesha and Mercury nakshatras are at the ending of cycles where the psychology of an individual changes. Mercury is the celestial bridge between higher forces and the Earth. Here Mercury helps you give up an attachment to the eternal soul and make a life on Earth. Before you are willing to do so however, you need to know why? What is hard to realise is that the more you search and analyse the truth, the more you get sucked into worldliness and lose your free spirit. So far the soul has dipped its feet in materialism, like a tourist enjoying its stay but not making a permanent residency. At the stage of Ashlesha the commitment to living on Earth has to be made. Every soul struggles to make this commitment and Mercury (the intellect) creates such struggles. But when the inevitability of this changeover is accepted, you can look beyond the struggles and expand your horizons. Mercury is easily influenced and the individual can go through many changes of personality as a child. What one should avoid is taking on the negative qualities.

Never underestimate the power of Ashlesha, or the poisons it carries within it. But don't underestimate its strengths either. Knowing your weaknesses and dealing with them is the greatest strength for Ashlesha and creates power. Ignoring your weaknesses or giving in to them creates a monster, the karmic knot that won't unravel.

The Moon is usually troubled as it struggles with the transformations of Ashlesha. In India astrologers do not like the Moon in Ashlesha and relate it only to the poisonous aspect. They name jealousy, possessiveness, vindictiveness... but forget the inspirational qualities of Ashlesha – knowledge, profundity and mysticism. The Moon remains troubled regardless of the path chosen as Ashlesha is all about transformation. While we may not be able to change what happened in childhood, we can use the positive Ashlesha energy to transform the 'now'.

The end of Ashlesha is Gandanta, the karmic knot where most of the toxins and poisons of Cancer are collected. Ashlesha is where the mind comes to terms with where they are, and has to deal with all the accumulated debris of previous lives. This Gandanta knot of Cancer is created by action, when we did not know the future price we would be paying. There were many new adventures from Aries to Cancer (Ashwini to Ashlesha) but now the soul has to recognise them and pay for the excesses. So Ashlesha can also be highly spiritual and cleansing.

Magha
00°00 to 13°20 Leo

Magha means 'mighty' or 'great'. People born in this nakshatra aspire towards eminence and are usually prominent in their chosen field. Leo also wants to establish its power and Magha relates to that. Magha is the second nakshatra ruled by Ketu, therefore representing the second cycle of the soul's journey. The nakshatras Magha to Jyeshta indicate the soul's full involvement in the pleasures and pains of earthly life through relationships, love, children, family life and emotional involvement. Leo desires freedom but also wants to be important and great. These qualities are both fulfilled in Magha. As in the first nakshatra dealing with material involvement, the soul still retains its divine connection. The desire is to be mighty and strong yet stay true to the soul. This can make these people extremely idealistic yet easily misunderstood, as others question their idealism when they are so materialistic.

The shadow planet Ketu rules Magha. Ketu is the tail of the celestial snake; a tail that carries both the past life karmas and the potential of man. It has no head, therefore it reacts instinctively and emotionally. Ketu's role in a birth chart is to look at the bigger picture. Once you stop being restricted by the conscious mind and make a fusion between the consciousness and the subconscious your world is open to all sorts of mysteries. The real struggle of Magha is in bringing visionary ideas to this world then having the desire to create a reality from them. The Magha Moon can be a visionary, one who has the ability to change the way the world thinks, as yet they are idealistic and not fully influenced by the materialistic world. Ketu, the significator of spiritual realisation ruling the commencing point of the materialistic journey, shows that it is the enjoyment of life that is part of the soul's divine mission.

Ketu as the first dasha is never easy. The conflict between idealism and practicality, mundane and spiritual, desires and moksha, can make these people feel torn in two and never sure where their loyalty lies. They should not feel guilty about their material needs but bring their idealism down to earth, follow their instincts and be true to their soul.

Purva Phalguni
13°20 to 26°40 Leo

The free soul now wants to procreate in its own image. This is the primary message of Leo and Purva Phalguni, that creation also leads to restriction, as these creations become responsibilities. The quality of what you create depends on past karmas.

Phal means fruit and *guni* is connected to gunas (good qualities). *Phalguni* is the nakshatra which brings the fruit of our good deeds from past lives into the present. *Purva* means first, indicating it is the former part of the two Phalguni nakshatras. Purva and Uttara Phalguni are parts of a whole nakshatra of four stars, which together resemble a bed. They indicate a similar purpose with very specific differences. Purva Phalguni is considered the lucky nakshatra, the good luck that is found from creating a lineage and having children. Here it is important to remember that even those who do not have children can be creative in other ways, with ideas, knowledge and wisdom, which can be used to influence future generations. In ancient times the child kept your name alive so it was important to establish a dynasty.

Venus rules Purva Phalguni. The Sanskrit name for Venus is *shukra* or semen so Shukra directly relates to procreation. Both sexes of Purva Phalguni are very fond of children and are good parents. Children were considered to represent divine creativity and their birth understood as the ability for a human to harness this natural power. The establishment of the family unit and perpetuating humanity are important and the Purva Phalguni Moon generates relationships to marry and start a family. It also helps you express creativity in artistic areas like drama, films, TV, music, show business, design and painting.

Purva Phalguni is the place for the soul to rest and enjoy what material life has to offer, to sup at the font of its pleasures. But this rest also involves it with the attractions of life. The Moon is happy to be involved in the worldliness; to create and find security within the family. This also shows a happy childhood spent enjoying the Venus dasha. Venus has to be extremely negative to take away the comforts and joy of Purva Phalguni.

Uttara Phalguni
26°40 to 30°00 Leo, 0°00 to 10°00 Virgo

Uttara Phalguni spans two signs, Leo and Virgo, and this changes the way it operates. In Leo there is a sense of achievement, of comforts that are yours by right, while in Virgo it starts to question these desires. There is only one pada of this nakshatra in Leo, the other three pada belong to Virgo. In my view there is a sense of perfection in this nakshatra. Whatever the path, difficult or enjoyable, the person deals with it.

Uttara Phalguni is the continuation of Purva Phalguni, the male energy to Purva's female. It represents the other half of the picture. *Phal* means fruit and *guni* is connected to the gunas (good qualities) so Phalguni is the nakshatra that brings the fruit of our good deeds from past lives into the present. *Uttara* means 'higher' indicating it is the latter part of the Phalguni nakshatras. Uttara Phalguni starts to question the need for involvement in materialism whereas Purva was happy just to be in it.

The Sun rules Uttara Phalguni. The Sun signifies creation and carries the knowledge of individual karma while also bearing authority, power, vitality and strength. Uttara Phalguni can feel isolated at times as other people may feel overshadowed by their light. People often do not recognise Uttara Phalguni's need for love.

Uttara Phalguni is famous for its leadership qualities; its chivalry, honour and nobility, and for maintaining the traditions, custom and religion in the rules of society. These people are interested in politics and the rules of living in a spiritual way. Uttara Phalguni in Leo gives a sense of divine right, the need to be and experience the good qualities in a socially acceptable manner, to forge alliances and to enjoy life. In Virgo the concept of how far we must enjoy life is examined. The new environment through which the soul has to travel is pure and unpolluted and the soul becomes aware that its immediate environment will get polluted by its own actions. This does create a greater psychological trauma for the Moon: To behave in the right way, to follow the social laws, to integrate with the society, to be noble, to have lofty ideals… But as we all know it isn't easy to live up to high flown concepts. Virgo Uttara Phalguni always feels it is not living up to its exacting standards. The discussions and analysis of how this is best to be done can sometimes totally obscure their larger vision.

Their first dasha of the Sun can be good but these people need to learn about social rules. What Uttara Phalguni must understand is that they can make their world a much better place to live in, but they should make realistic rules with which they can live their life.

Hasta
10°00 to 23°20 Virgo

Hasta means 'hand'. The hand reflects the destiny of an individual and the individual effort. The left and right hands are negative and positive, female and male energies, past and future lives. The hand is an entire field of knowledge and Hasta can know everything, or at least thinks it does. This is the aspect that can give immense power or restrict personal growth.

Hasta people feel that by controlling the flow of their destiny they can become what the soul wants them to be, and thereby achieve their soul's desire. But they can sometimes limit themselves to material desires only, not understanding the bigger picture. Hasta people do not want to leave anything to chance, they want to be in control of what is around them, they accept only what they can understand. They think they can change their destiny by harnessing and directing their own power but the inability to do so makes them frustrated. The real vision of Hasta should be limitless and universal not limited to one's own world.

The Moon rulership of this nakshatra makes for changing perspectives and moving realities. Hasta people can be moody and reflect the waxing and waning phases of the Moon. Although they appear confident and in control, their inner self is vulnerable, insecure and in conflict. Hasta is the nakshatra of the mind, with both the Moon and Mercury as main influences. If they do not have the mind in control they can be mentally troubled; thinking too much is both their strength and weakness. They are great thinkers and good at words but usually troubled as the mind is not at peace.

The Moon as the first dasha can be fun. These people develop their intellect soon but must learn to control their wayward mind.

Chitra
23°40 to 30°00 Virgo, 00°00 to 06°40 Libra

Chitra means an image, a reflection or a beautiful picture. The connection is to illusions rather than reality. These people can embrace illusions as reality, thereby immersing themselves in materialistic life. Materialism is considered the greatest illusion according to vedic philosophy. The beautiful picture is the revelation of the soul, and the soul within is divine and pure regardless of the illusion they have embraced. The story of the Moon in Chitra is about the revelation of its true potential. But the process of finding your hidden self can be extremely painful.

Chitra spans Virgo and Libra. Virgo represents the perfectionist stage and Libra where it strives for balance. This is where the soul starts seeing the reflection of itself. There are usually two types of Chitra people, those who do not recognise anything beyond this world as a reality, and those who have suddenly come face to face with their soul and started to move towards re-establishing the connection.

Mars rules Chitra, and Mars is a dynamic planet with plenty of courage. This is needed as the search for the true personality is never easy. The Moon will need to see the true picture and this takes time. At first the desires and ambitions dominate, the person can appear lazy, selfish and stuck in the world of tamas, but Chitra Moons are aware that there is more to life than meets the eye. Mars gives some of them the courage and confidence to externalise their potential regardless of the personal cost. As the latent talents are externalised, the second type of Chitra emerges – one who is selfless and truly beautiful.

The Chitra Moon does not give an easy childhood as Mars is the first dasha followed by Rahu. The Rahu dasha in childhood is never easy as Rahu can increase the negative qualities of Chitra and immerse them in a world of illusion. It will be only later in life that Chitra people truly find themselves.

Swati
06°40 to 20°00 Libra

Swati means 'sword'. Swati carries the sword as a tool for self-advancement, cutting through competition and obstacles in its path. Swati is also the name of the wife of the Sun, so Swati also personified self-existence, the principle of relying on yourself and worldly connections. Sometimes Swati forgets its spiritual purpose and gets involved in worldly pleasures and pains. Relationships and success in world matters become of prime importance and these people can forget their connection with the universal soul. Swati wants to create its own world, with its own rules, and forget the world beyond consciousness. And as such these people can develop a hard surface and appear insensitive. Swati Moon people live in their world and have the ability to influence those around them, but they shouldn't forget that others can influence their well-made environment.

Swati is where the Sun reaches its exact debilitation point, and so it appears that the soul is cut off from its higher self. But this is a wrong assumption; the soul has to immerse itself in worldly pursuits before it can decide to move on to the next important step of spiritual growth. This is the debt it has to pay for being born on Earth. Swati promotes self reliance while still trying to find a balance between spiritual and material needs.

The shadowy Rahu rules Swati. Rahu forms just the head of the demon; therefore it has no body. It thinks and forgets to feel. This instils a strong identification with the outer personality. Personality, self reliance and personal ego are all where people forget to be in touch with their emotions or their soul. As the first dasha ruler Rahu will encourage a person towards ambition and success, yet not much satisfies them. Rahu dasha at a young age is never easy, as a person can be chasing many shadows and not catch any of them.

Vishakha
20°00 to 30°00 Libra, 00°00 to 03°20 Scorpio

Visha means to enter and *kha* means heaven. Vishakha is standing at the gates, aspiring to cross the threshold into heaven and find the route back to the soul, striving to break away from the layers of materialism that surround the soul. This leads to a transformation for the Vishakha Moon. Vishakha people are at a stage where the soul is standing at the threshold of higher experiences, willing and able to take on board new lessons that change their outlook on life, but the change does not take place without great churning of emotions. The feeling that heaven is always somewhere else creates dissatisfaction with current circumstances.

Vishakha spans two signs, it is mostly in Libra with one pada in Scorpio. The main difference between the Libra and Scorpio Vishakha is that in Libra, there is a struggle to juggle the material and the spiritual and find meaning in the two differing realities now present, whereas the Scorpio Vishakha finds it impossible to locate a balance. While Libra allows an individual to live a life materially while recognising the spiritual soul, Scorpio Vishakha gives no option. Scorpio needs to transform but can remain stuck in its old ways. The Moon is debilitated here so is very troubled especially if there is a refusal to change and transform. These people have to be careful that they are not dominated by their weaknesses (jealousy, possessiveness, bitterness, envy etc). The complexities of Vishakha bring the soul to find inspiration from their darkness and discover the divinity within.

Jupiter rules Vishakha. The first dasha for Vishakha is usually comfortable and happy but the emotional struggles begin soon. The dasha that follows Jupiter is Saturn and depending on the length of the Jupiter dasha, Saturn can suddenly bring childhood to an end as it brings responsibilities to the Vishakha Moon. As these people aspire to touch the heavens, they can achieve a lot materially but it leaves a residual sense of dissatisfaction. Jupiter brings the wisdom that helps expand horizons to go beyond the present and this nakshatra combines the qualities of Jupiter and Venus, both gurus and both giving deep wisdom if the inner voice is listened to. Other people will always seek the advice of Vishaka, but these people are not always able to be a good advisor to themselves. The need for a guru to fathom the mysteries of life is essential.

Anuradha
03°20 to 16°40 Scorpio
Anuradha is a beautiful nakshatra living within the apparent darkness of Scorpio, showing that light can shine anywhere. *Anuradha* means a 'small flash of lightning' or 'a tiny spark', suggesting that it only takes a small flash of intuition or a tiny spark of consciousness to make us aware of what we really want from life. This opens our mind to our path to happiness. This spark can be lit regardless of present circumstances. People can aspire to their divinity in whatever situation they are in and should never lose hope or consider life hopeless. All it takes is a little spark, that ignites the fire of spirituality and personal progress towards the soul. In fact the vedic myths are full of demons who changed their personality completely when they discovered their tiny spark.

Anuradha is connected to the lotus. The lotus plant seeds in the mud and as it flowers it appears to reach towards the Sun. Once it has flowered it withers away and returns back to the mud where it will root again to repeat the whole process. The lotus is said to flower so that it can be laid at the feet of the gods, just as the soul is born to experience life and death so that it can break away from this to find enlightenment. It illustrates the evolutionary aspect of the soul, that reaches to the Sun (universal consciousness) from the mud (ignorance and soul concealed in matter). Its withering away symbolises death, and its rebirth is the process of re-rooting and flowering. Anuradha aspires to reach the soul and will keep on attempting to make the effort regardless of however many times it fails. This inspiration allows Anuradha people to take themselves out of any situation and transform. The most important thing for them is to remain positive and inspired towards their goal even when faced with hardships. As long as they have the goal, they light their spark and grow towards the light.

The Anuradha Moon must keep aspiring for the best. It has moved away from the exact degree of debilitation and is therefore now more comfortable with its path. Saturn, the great teacher of cosmic truths, rules Anuradha. His influence is tough to deal with as he teaches responsibility, restriction, and the ability to endure life in the hope of finding the light that will guide to self-realisation. All these messages from Saturn at the beginning of life give Anuradha Moon the ability to bear pain, and these people tend to take on burdens from a young age. Mars, the sign ruler, wants to act but Saturn keeps restricting. This causes a great deal of friction until these contrary energies are harnessed and used properly. Anuradha Moon people can feel blocked until they learn to restrain their natural desires. Their greatest weakness is idealism and unrealistic expectations of love and relationships. Their ability to love for the sake of love can bring disappointments, but Saturn helps them learn about detachment.

Jyeshta
16°40 to 30°00 Scorpio

Jyeshta means elder sister, the middle finger, or the holy river Ganges. The elder sister is looked upon with great respect as she is like one's mother, the middle finger is the finger of destiny, and the river Ganges is said to wash away all our negative karma. The symbol of Jyeshta is the earring, which signifies occult status. The earring was given to divine kings who had mastered their lower nature and gained occult powers that allowed them to rule the world, communicate with spirits, and have the knowledge of past and future lives. This is the potential contained within Jyeshta.

Jyeshta also has a darker meaning. She is the sister of the bountiful goddess of luck, Laxmi, but she represents the opposite. Jyeshta is considered the goddess of bad luck. It does not mean that those born in Jyeshta are unlucky but they must not be the creators of their own misfortune.

The Moon is Jyeshta is very troubled as it navigates complex situations. Scorpio shows the soul split into two, the material desires running rampant and the spiritual desires equally strong. These people find it difficult to make a bridge between the two. At Jyeshta, the polarisation becomes even more intense as this is the last nakshatra of materialistic tendencies. Desires are at their highest intensity yet there is a deep need for change. These people learn about kundalini, occult, and secret knowledge in a bid to master their hidden demons. They have a voracious appetite for life, and this becomes their weakness, though sometimes taking or consuming their weakness to the extreme leads to change. Jyeshta people feel very powerful, believing they can control themselves and that different rules apply to them, but this arrogance makes them create their own bad luck, their own demons. It can produce baggage throughout their life until they do prayaschit, making amends and turning towards a more spiritual journey.

The ruler of Jyeshta is Mercury and Jyeshta represents the struggle of the mind to adapt to the new reality of life. The first dasha in early childhood may not show the angst of Jyeshta but there can be issues connected to the mother or the relationship with the mother that influences their whole life. The Moon in the last degrees of Jyeshta is in a Gandanta, a very difficult position. Here the storms of transformation are intense and life will transform at a very young age as the dasha changes from Mercury to Ketu. The end of Mercury dashas always carry negativity or karmic poisons and to face these issues in childhood is usually difficult. It may be through relationship with the mother or the family that you have to deal with the rejections of Ketu.

Mula
00°00 to 13°20 Sagittarius
Mula is the start of the final part of the soul's mission towards finding eternal happiness or moksha. *Mula* means root and it is connected to the *muladhara chakra* (the repository of latent spiritual energy). Mula suggests that we are the root of all our problems as well as the blessings of our good fortune. These people are rooted in the physical, the objective and the material while their aspirations may be for the subtle and psychic. Their dissatisfaction with life will lessen if they realise that a tree needs strong roots to grow upwards. The Mula Moon needs to be practical and

build strong foundations before it can move towards the spiritual journey. A spiritual aspirant must have strong roots in belief, a strong support network, and this provides the ideal environment to develop and move towards the higher knowledge. But the Mula Moon does not find life easy.

Mula is the final nakshatra ruled by Ketu, the significator for *moksha* or self-realisation. The soul is born on Earth to enjoy life but not to get attached to it. Its final aim is moksha, liberation from the cycles of life and death. Mula aspire for freedom and release from the burden of responsibilities and this usually makes them careless about their practical responsibilities. Ketu can make these people reject their roots, but how can a tree grow or prosper without its roots? Jupiter brings spiritual wisdom and Ketu represents the past – if only they can reconcile with the past then true wisdom can flourish. If we accept today, we can be happy with tomorrow. Mula is never easy as it begins life with Ketu and at that early stage people are not able to handle its impact. Gandanta Mula usually has the hardest struggles.

Purva Ashadha
13°20 to 26°40 Sagittarius

Purva means first, indicating it is the former part of the two Ashadha nakshatras. *Ashadha* means what we cannot suppress. The true nature of man comes out regardless of how we try to conceal it. Purva Ashadha is linked to the following nakshatra Uttara Ashadha, and together they represent the common principle of unfolding new talents and spirituality. In Purva Ashadha there are still some blocks to expressing the nature fully while Uttara Ashadha embraces the changes.

Purva Ashadha Moon people are creative, talented, bright and intelligent. Venus, the planetary ruler, bestows talent in the arts, crafts, music and drama. Many creative geniuses are born under this sign. Jupiter and Venus, the two gurus of the zodiac, influence this nakshatra, making it wise both in a worldly and spiritual sense. The first dasha of Venus is usually comfortable; these people do not suffer the difficulties and angst of Mula. However successful they may be in their chosen career, they will always be humble and self-effacing. Yet they can be plagued by self doubt as their aspire for perfection and ultimate happiness and the greatest expression of their talents. Life is as yet limited by their humanness; life on Earth does not grant self-realisation easily and at the stage of Purva Ashadha the revelation of talents and latent spirituality can take place if they do shy away from their material path.

This nakshatra is the balance between spiritual and material. Spirituality is now a reality but they must still work in a material world and it is how they balance this that will make them either profoundly influential or troubled and out of sync. The Moon represents water and purity and both are easy to pollute. The mind can become corrupted or polluted if they are not careful and subject to change through transforming life experiences. The mind is usually unsettled in Sagittarius as the Moon rules the 8th sign from it and they must learn to embrace this change.

Uttara Ashadha
26°40 to 30°00 Sagittarius, 00°00 to 10°00 Capricorn
Uttara means higher and *Ashadha* means unrestrained. It indicates what cannot be suppressed. Together the two Ashadhas represent the unfolding of new spirituality. In Purva Ashadha there was the dawning of new realities, but the assimilation into the psyche takes place in Uttara Ashadha. Uttara Ashadha people are creative and talented like their cosmic other half, but they have moved on spiritually so their journey is more internal. Their creativity is not always expressed artistically as philosophically

Uttara Ashadha people realise that to move forward spiritually they need to control their desires. It does not matter whether they are rich or poor, Uttara Ashadha learns to do with little. They are not so obsessed by material things any longer and voluntarily embrace austerity. They are moving away from sensuality and comfort and adopting a simple life even when involved in materialistic pursuits. The Moon has a hard time embracing the austere regime of Uttara Ashadha. In Sagittarius it can be easier than in Capricorn.

Uttara Ashadha shows the struggle of man to find his own lost light, lost in layers of material desires. There has to be a true understanding of the inner light otherwise these people can think they are devoid of higher possibilities and remain concerned with material things. Uttara Ashadha is a lonely nakshatra. All its symbolism is connected to being alone. These people are moving away from sensuality and adopting a simple life even when they are materially wealthy.

The Sun rules Uttara Ashadha and the first dasha of the Sun can give an uneasy relationship with the father or expressing the divine self, and this is carried in the psyche throughout life. These people want power yet they need to be democratic about it. Uttara Ashadha should always go for positions where they are doing good for others. They are paying off their past karma so that they are lighter at the end of it.

Shravana
10°00 to 23°20 Capricorn

Shravana means listening, especially to the scriptures. In ancient times the scriptures were retold orally from teacher to student so Shravana was an important part of the spiritual seeker's discipline. Shravana develops a technique of being able to hear in the silence, and listening to the sounds of silence can only be achieved through self-discipline and meditation. We can only hear the true meaning of the scriptures when there is silence of the mind and we begin to hear new meanings for words that we were not aware of before. To sit in silence we have to like ourselves; it forces us to recognise the truth and not hide behind the cacophony of life. Shravana begins a new stage in the soul's aspiration for spirituality. From Mula to Uttara Ashadha the soul makes the necessary changes and unearths its desire for the spirituality that had been hidden away. Now it will take proper steps to embrace and nurture the spirituality by imbibing wisdom.

The Moon rules Shravana and the nakshatra is in Capricorn ruled by Saturn. This Saturn Moon combination makes for a difficult situation. The Moon waxes and wanes, is emotional and changeable while Saturn is disciplined, rigid and inflexible. The mind dominates every aspect of life. Here Shravana aspires to control the mind, to be in charge of it instead of the mind ruling and creating uncertainty. Saturn teaches the control of emotions, to be detached from the ups and downs of life, to learn to enjoy both the pleasures and the pain with equal regard. Do not allow sorrow to make you sad neither allow happiness to make you too happy. If you distance yourself from both and do not allow the extreme ends of emotions to affect you any longer, you are truly learning to control the mind and being in charge of life. Shravana forces you to take more responsibility for yourself as you experience inner growth and move towards higher knowledge.

The first dasha is of the Moon, which offers an easier childhood. This can be quite studious with a thirst for knowledge and this is a nakshatra that needs knowledge and silence. Even if they did not develop it earlier in life, these people should aim for knowledge and silence as it will make them feel complete.

Dhanishta
23°20 to 30°00 Capricorn, 00°00 to 06°40 Aquarius

Dhani means wealthy and *ishta* means complete. Together *Dhanishta* means complete wealth. Dhanishta is wealthy in mind and spirit. In ancient texts when the sages alluded to a person being wealthy, they meant the wealth of good character, thoughts and actions. This was considered far superior to mere material wealth. Dhanishta is the nakshatra where the soul assimilates all that it has developed so far and protects it from the outside influences of materialism. The soul knows it is spiritually wealthy, and this is the nakshatra where it becomes comfortable with these thoughts. Spiritual wealth may not come easily to Dhanishta, but it can be assimilated through selfless work, letting go of the personal ego and working with compassion and high ideals for universal good. These people have to fight for their rights, but also do a lot of service for others.

Dhanishta spans two signs, Capricorn and Aquarius, both ruled by Saturn. Dhanishta is very different in Capricorn than it is in Aquarius. Capricorn Dhanishta will want to be responsible for life, to do its duty, and it can be so easy for them to get involved in what others want to do – their family, friends, children or parents – that they lose what they want themselves. Aquarius Dhanishta is more inclined towards a world vision, caring for others and taking on a responsibility for the world. Earth issues, environment, politics are on top of their agenda.

The ruling planet Mars is the planet of courage and action. Mars allows a single-minded pursuit of dharmic responsibility. Dhanishta have to conquer their inner demons and outer enemies (material desires), and Mars is a warrior whose main role here is to defend against negative desires and all the forces that stifle soul growth. Mars will show immense courage to guard the soul while it assimilates its new spiritual direction. While Mars as a first dasha is good, Rahu immediately follows it so Dhanishta people usually have an unusual start to life. They may feel outsiders even if they are leading conventional lives.

Shatabhishak
06°40 to 20°00 Aquarius

Shatabhishak can have many meanings. *Shat* means hundred and *bhishak* means demons. *Abhishak* means healers. The nakshatra can be both demonic and godly and highlights the good and evil, both sides of man. These people are perpetually fighting the negative forces within, wanting to control their inner demons so that they can aspire towards the divine. What happens in Shatabhishak is that the demons/weaknesses keep coming up, forcing us to deal with them. It is only when the weaknesses are conquered and we control the negative forces that we become truly divine.

Shatabhishak seeks divine guidance to leads them from darkness to light. Their aspirations are idealistic and great, but not all can reach such lofty heights. Most struggle to control their inner demons and try to hide them from the world, thinking they will be judged and found wanting. It is the secrecy and attempts to hide part of their true nature that gets Shatabhishak into trouble, not their weaknesses.

Shatabhishak can be self-destructive to start with. Once they train the negative energy to become a positive force, the inner poisons get healed and the mind awakens to a glorious new world where they have the capacity to defy gravity, convention, and make immense changes to the way of thinking. Shatabhishak have to learn control and become masters of their destiny.

The Moon in Shatabhishak can be like a shadow, elusive and unreliable. As people try to chase shadows, they realise they are intangible, and consequently that they may never really know a Shatabhishak person. Thus Shatabhishak Moons feel lonely and isolated yet are responsible for this loneliness themselves. As they are unable to confide in others, they feel they are not as good as others think they are. Their need to hide makes them unreliable; so others do not trust them. The first dasha of Rahu would be tough to deal with as it carries fears within the psyche of not being able to complete the divine mission. This is never an easy nakshatra to work with unless you understand its higher vibrations.

Purva Bhadra
20°00 to 30°00 Aquarius, 00°00 to 03°20 Pisces

Purva means first and *bhadra* has many meanings including beautiful, auspicious, blessed, gracious and happy. The blessings usually come from good deeds in past lives, now being experienced as good luck. The Indian meaning of good luck is not connected to financial wealth alone. Good fortune means having good family, excellent relationships, wonderful children and a good life where knowledge and wisdom guide you to find your true beauty. This is not physical beauty, but the loveliness of a good soul and spiritual inner being. Here we cannot doubt the idealism of the soul but these people make simple mistakes as they work towards their spiritual goal. It is not a place they have ever been before so they can be over-enthusiastic in their zeal to get the message across.

Purva Bhadra is connected to Uttara Bhadra. While having distinct personalities, they form a singular principle that is split into two opposing forces. Jupiter rules Purva and Saturn rules Uttara. Together they represent the Sun and Moon, darkness and light, fire and water, heat and cold, masculine and feminine. Purva Bhadra is mostly in Aquarius with just one pada in Pisces. This is where the final push for self-realisation takes place. The soul is extremely mature yet can make immature mistakes as it attempts to be at one with the cosmic plan. The Aquarius waters are flowing, broken from the restraints of Shatabhishak and as the nakshatras come towards their end, the soul becomes more drawn towards spirituality. These people have to pay extra attention to their material issues as the soul has still to live in the world.

With Purva Bhadra in Aquarius, Saturn rules the sign and Jupiter the nakshatra, while in Pisces both the sign and nakshatra are ruled by Jupiter. Jupiter stands for expansion, happiness and higher knowledge, the positive fruits of past karma bringing conditions of affluence, comfort and happiness. Jupiter's main concern is to give you a good material life so you can concentrate on the essential spiritual development. Saturn and Jupiter represent the duality between expansion and restriction, which finally makes for the eternal balance. In Aquarius, Saturn will still stop Purva Bhadra from achieving all its aims. There are still responsibilities to be fulfilled for humanity, ego issues to be worked out, the material life continues to have a say here. The soul must be conscious of its karmic responsibilities. Jupiter becomes a guide during this tough balancing act, whereas Pisces Purva Bhadra feels no restrictions.

Neither will the Moon know the entire picture. It will try to find the answers and be very strong minded about what it understands, but the duality of Purva Bhadra can make these people lack confidence. They are spiritual yet adventurous, seeking to find the answers of what to do with their new found spirituality. This can be a problem for practical purposes as this is not a very materialistic Moon. The first dasha will be of Jupiter, which is usually good, but Saturn follows it. Depending on how long the Jupiter dasha is, Purva Bhadra can soon experience the restrictions of Saturn and learn about the two sides of its nature. There are still some worldly issues to resolve before it can totally submerge itself in being one with the divine.

Uttara Bhadra
03°20 to 16°40 Pisces

Uttara Bhadra is an extension of the previous nakshatra, Purva Bhadra. While having distinct personalities, they form a singular principle that is split into two opposing forces. (See Purva Bhadra above). Saturn rewards all the trials and tribulations in Uttara Bhadra so it has a deeper understanding of what the bigger picture means. For a moment it enjoys being involved in the world of materialism, refining its attachments and letting go of these last residuals before it totally transforms itself.

Uttara means higher and *bhadra* has many meanings including beautiful, auspicious, blessed, gracious and happy. All aspects highlight the positive qualities that Uttara Bhadra is blessed with. The blessings usually come from good deeds in past lives, which are now being experienced as good luck. Here there is a detachment from both the pleasure and pains of life. Uttara Bhadra has to be careful it does not revel in the pain of life; these people have a high threshold for pain and can make themselves victims to situations they think to be their final test before they find their ideal. Often Uttara Bhadra people remain in tough relationships/situations far longer than they need to.

Uttara Bhadra Moon understands about blessings on a higher, more subtle plane. The soul wants more than just the ordinary. Saturn who rules Uttara Bhadra is the great teacher of cosmic truths but his influence is tough to deal with. Uttara Bhadra has the blessing to use the lessons of Saturn in the best possible way and faced with such powerful karmic forces they have to dig deep into their inner resources. The first dasha of

Saturn can cause frustration, even misery in childhood and teens, as it restricts the natural energy from expanding. With maturity, if these people learn to use the Saturn forces properly, they start on the path towards self-realisation. Saturn here deals with karma on a very subtle level. There can still be some mental blocks, the feeling of karmic debts still to be paid, and a few unfulfilled desires that are blocking the final doorway to the higher self. As this is the 26th nakshatra, the total involvement in the divine is denied as there is work to be completed on the earthly plane.

Revati
16°40 to 30°00 Pisces
Revati means abundant or wealthy. This can also be spiritual wealth as Revati is the nourisher. In the puranas she is the wife of Mitra, a form of the Sun god, providing nourishment to the soul while it struggles with the great implications of finding itself. Once we find the seed of creation within us and connect with the divine, life cannot remain the same. Major changes and transformations happen as this seed grows into another future.

Being the last nakshatra of the zodiac, Revati has the power to realise ultimate truths about life, love, relationships, transformation, change and death. Not everyone is meant to be so highly spiritual and this becomes the main struggle for Revati individuals as they want moksha, they aspire for the ideal, so can feel out of touch with the present. They can be generous, yet feel misunderstood. They can be let down by society and the world as it fails to live up to their ideal.

Mercury rules Revati. According to the vedic myths, Mercury is the son of the Moon. The Moon is the subconscious mind and Mercury is the rational, practical conscious mind, but it is still a fragment of total consciousness. What Mercury perceives as reality, is only a small part of the ultimate reality. Mercury rules the ending cycles of the nakshatras, where the change of individual consciousness takes place by understanding and going beyond the limitations of intellect. The Revati Moon is at an end of a major cycle of soul development where the consciousness meets the intellect to form new realities for the future.

The Revati Moon is idealistic and wants to nourish others. These people can feel their life is full of disappointments if they do not understand their spiritual path. They can also lack skills for the material world which can make them feel insecure especially if other areas of their life indicate materialistic ambitions. They will try to be excellent in whatever they do, but unless their aim is spiritual they may feel a failure. The first dasha of Mercury can be quite good unless the person is born at the end of Revati on a Gandanta point. Then it indicates major changes right from birth and the insecurities of Revati can be quite pronounced if they are born with the Moon in Gandanta.

The Role of Saturn and Rahu

Saturn is the lord of vayu and Rahu also has influence on it at a subtle level. Whereas in other bhutas vayu needs to be strong, here it needs to be kept quiet as if it is strong it can be destructive. The winds of the mind should be like gentle breezes not like violent storms. Saturn or Rahu can directly influence the Moon by conjunctions, aspects or by their transits. Saturn has many difficult transits directly connected to the Moon – sade sati, ashtama shani (including the 64th navamsha) and kantaka shani. Shani is the Sanskrit name for Saturn.

Rahu will make an impact through eclipses as well. Saturn aspects the 3rd, 7th and 10th houses and Rahu aspects the 5th, 7th and 9th houses from themselves; if they aspect the Moon, they will create disturbances.

During the time when the vayu is disturbed, doing yoga, meditation and chanting is a good remedy. This is not a time to make decisions or decide on major life matters.

Sade Sati – Saturn's Long Transit

This is a seven and a half year transit of Saturn over the 12th, 1st, and 2nd houses from your natal moon. Sade sati usually indicates a complete transformation of life. Your priorities are going to change and possibly your career or direction.

Sade sati is the most important of Saturn's transits, so you need to be aware when it is going to be experienced. I cannot over-emphasise the importance of this transit. It is a 7½ year transit, and it is most powerful when Saturn goes over the nakshatra and pada where the Moon is placed. This is the time when the vayu is high and the mind is disturbed. Often a major issue needs to be dealt with but as the mind is so confused as the vayu has risen, it is difficult to see the wood from the trees –

mistakes are possible. Doing a Saturn fast and the relevant remedial measures as detailed in Chapter 8 are important.

Kantaka Shani

Kantaka Shani is Saturn transiting the 4th house from the Moon. This is usually a difficult transit involving home, children and relationships.

Ashtama Shani

Ashtama Shani is Saturn transiting the 8th house from the Moon. This can lead to intense difficulties with partnerships and is usually a time to re-negotiate partnership issues. As it can sometimes lead to a break up this is not a good time to enter into partnerships. Health issues may also come to the fore. There can be an unexpected event that can lead to major life changes.

64th Navamsha

The 64th navamsha is a difficult point in the chart and its ruler is regarded as a malefic planet. This navamsha is usually calculated from the Moon: count round to the 8th house exactly by degree and you will come to the 64th navamsha.

In a chart where the Moon is at 4° Aries (Ashwini Nakshatra, Taurus pada), its 64th navamsha will be where 4° Scorpio (Anuradha nakshatra, Leo pada) falls. The ruler of the 64th Navamsha from the Moon is the Sun. This navamsha is a sensitive point for transit and the rulers of the 64th navamsha will create problems during their dasha and bhuktis. When a malefic transit – usually Saturn or Rahu – passes over this point in your chart, then you are going to experience health issues, emotional problems, breakup in relationships, or unexpected changes.

Rahu's Impact through Solar and Lunar Eclipses

Solar and lunar eclipses usually fall six months apart and bring some kind of transformation.

To the ancient sages the eclipses, especially solar, meant that the light from the sun had vanished, and the deadly silence and disturbance of birds and animals made them fear that the end was coming. As the dark shadow of the Moon engulfed the Sun, it appeared as if a demon was swallowing it. An eclipse is always a portent for some change to come, a divine warning. The Sun sheds its light for a moment and exposes the shadow of the Moon, which is Rahu, and when Rahu is revealed, our hidden side comes to the surface. An unusual aspect of our consciousness is shown, highlighting a different way of life.

In my experience eclipses are indications of a change – for better or worse. During eclipses, Rahu is disturbing the vayu element of the mind and creating mental anxiety. This disturbance becomes more acute when the eclipse is close to the Moon or an important planet or ascendant. When the mind is disturbed we are liable to make decisions that may not be helpful. Rather than try to decide on a course of action, we should be concentrating on calming the mind and retaining equilibrium.

Rahu's Transit over the Moon

When Rahu makes an exact transit over the Moon, the vayu bhuta rises too and the mind can become disturbed. For the duration of the transit (usually about one week), fears and anxieties can become heightened and the mind disturbed for no apparent reason.

The Nakshatra Analysis

Paul McCartney's nakshatra is Ashlesha. *Ashlesha* means to 'embrace' – the soul embracing life so that it can act out its karma. Mercury rules Ashlesha and Mercury nakshatras are at the ending of cycles where the psychology of an individual changes. This nakshatra indicates a great thinker, someone full of ideas. There are emotional struggles along the way as the mind does not want to make a commitment to life on Earth. In this case of a singer-songwriter, the Ashlesha mind would understand the trials and transformations of others, as Paul would have faced them himself. Ashlesha is inspirational and wise and as one of the leaders of the phenomenally successful 'Beatles', Paul McCartney inspired a whole generation and still continues to do so. When the group ended he was happy to transform into another group, 'Wings', and lead that successfully too till 1981. Since then he has been a solo artist. The loss of his wife Linda in 1998 would have been another transforming experience for him. Throughout his life he has been writing songs and been mentally creative and this is an important aspect of Ashlesha.

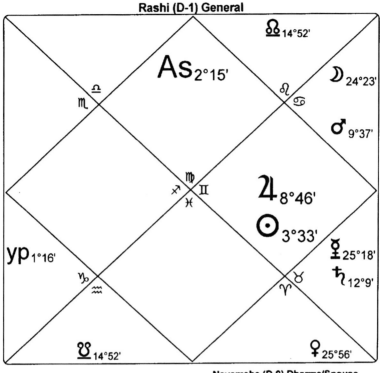

Rashi (D-1) General

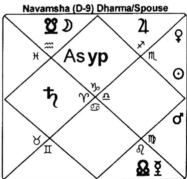

Navamsha (D-9) Dharma/Spouse

Paul McCartney
Songwriter, Composer, Ex-Beatle
Born 14.00 (War Time – 2.00) on
18 June 1942, Liverpool, England
Nakshatra – Ashlesha
First Dasha – Mercury
Nama – De
Nakshatra Bhuta – Apas
Nakshatra Gandanta – None

The Ashlesha Moon falls in the 11th house of profit and Paul McCartney has special skills in making money. His company owns the copyright of over 3000 songs and he is involved in other areas of the music business that has made him one of the richest artists in the UK.

The First Dasha and the Karmic Pattern of the Life

The dasha gives a life path to follow but one has flexibility within this; we can follow the path to the best or the worst of our abilities. As the dashas are connected to the Moon they show the changing needs of the mind. Paul's dashas have led him from Mercury to the present Rahu.

Paul McCartney's Dasha patterns

Dasha	From	To
Mercury	18 June 1942	14 Aug 1948
Ketu	14 Aug 1948	14 Aug 1956
Venus	14 Aug 1956	14 Aug 1976
Sun	14 Aug 1976	14 Aug 1982
Moon	14 Aug 1982	14 Aug 1992
Mars	14 Aug 1992	14 Aug 2002
Rahu	14 Aug 2002	14 Aug 2020

Paul McCartney began his life with a Mercury dasha. Mercury is retrograde and in the 9th house. It lasted till 14 Aug 1948 and this first dasha is very important as it leaves a permanent impression on the mind. Mercury is also the lagna lord and is placed in the 9th house of dharma and good fortune. It conjuncts Saturn, which is the 5th house ruler, and both the 5th and 9th houses are connected to writing and the higher mind. Paul McCartney is in the *Guinness Book of World Records* as the most successful musician and composer in the world with 60 gold discs and 100 million records sold so far.

He had a Ketu dasha till 1956, which would not have been an easy time for him. Ketu deals with past life karma and is usually tough to experience during childhood. He met George Harrison during this time on the way to school. This would be a past life connection.

The Venus dasha was his most productive as Venus deals with music and rules the 2nd house of voice and the lucky 9th house; but the dasha began with sadness as he lost his mother on 31 October 1956. Meeting John Lennon soon after, forming the Beatles and experiencing its ensuing success is the stuff of legend. He married Linda Eastman on 12 March 1969 in the Venus Jupiter dasha, and Jupiter rules his 7th house. The Beatles were finally dissolved after Paul filed a lawsuit in 1970 during the Venus Saturn dasha.

The Sun dasha from 1976 to 1982 was not the best time for him as he was generally criticised for the quality of his music. The Sun rules the 12th house of loss, and 12th house dashas are not usually productive.

The Moon dasha from 14 August 1982 to 14 August 1992 is in its own sign and in the 11th house of profit and this was when he went solo. He also collaborated with Stevie Wonder and Michael Jackson.

The Mars dasha ran from 14 August 1992 to 14 August 1999. Mars is the worst planet for a Virgo lagna; it is debilitated in his chart and its dasha brought the loss of his wife Linda from cancer on 17 April 1998 in the Mars Venus dasha. As well as being a very difficult time for him emotionally, he would also have felt angry. He met Heather Mills at the end of this dasha in February 1999, (although they made their relationship public later).

McCartney's Rahu dasha began on 14 August 1999. Rahu is in the 12th house of loss. He would have been extremely lonely at the beginning of this period after the loss of Linda, and would have been looking for companionship. The 12th house Rahu did not promise a happy outcome for his second marriage which took place on 11 June 2002 in Rahu Jupiter. (Jupiter rules his 7th house of relationships). Paul filed for divorce on 29 June 2006 in the Rahu Saturn dasha. This is an expensive divorce as the dasha ruler is in the 12th house and Paul did not sign a pre-nuptial agreement with Heather Mills.

The Role of Saturn and Rahu
Saturn and Rahu conjunctions, dashas or transits can make the vayu of the mind rise and if the individual is not careful, become troubled.

Paul McCartney does not have Saturn or Rahu conjunct the Moon. At present he is in a Rahu dasha and this dasha can be tough on the mind as Rahu is the co-ruler of vayu and can raise the mental stresses and block calmness or clarity. Sade sati is the most difficult of the Saturn transits as it makes the vayu and the mind stressed to the point where one makes wrong decisions. His marriage and divorce to Heather Mills are unfortunately all part of Saturn's great lesson. His sade sati began on 27 July 2002 and lasts till 9 September 2009. The marriage took place in June 2002 but emotional storms would have begun immediately after with the start of sade sati. When he announced his divorce on 29 June 2006, Saturn was in Cancer transiting near the natal Moon. The whole process of divorce from Heather Mills and the great tabloid frenzy it generated was taking place when Saturn was exactly transiting his Moon – this is considered the peak of the sade sati.

There is an important eclipse that Paul McCartney should be aware of – the solar eclipse on 7 Feb 2008 is at 23°54 Capricorn opposite his 24°23 Moon in Cancer. This may bring to light a new relationship or complete the ending process of his old one with Heather Mills. Rahu will transit over his Moon on 15 August 2008 – a time for him to be careful about the decisions he makes as he will find it hard to be focused.

Nama Nakshatra

The name given at birth should help calm the mind down if it is rightly chosen according to its nakshatras and pada. Paul's nama nakshatra should begin with 'de' according to the Moon in the third pada of Ashlesha. His first name beginning with 'P' connects to the 2nd pada of Chitra. Although 'pa' comes under Uttara Phalguni, the way Paul is pronounced it resounds with the 'po' of Chitra. Paul McCartney was christened James Paul McCartney, but as he never used James it would not be studied in this exercise. The second pada of Chitra is in Virgo which also happens to be Paul McCartney's ascendant – a very good choice for an internationally famous name. 'Jaa' falls in Uttara Ashadha which is Capricorn (5th house) so if he had decided to use his first name it would have been a good choice.

The Bhuta of the Nakshatra

His nakshatra bhuta is apas, which connects to the Swadhisthana chakra. Apas is creative, emotional and sensuous, and its rulership by Venus gives a natural affinity for the arts and music. Apas is mentally much calmer and can be instinctive and intuitive – qualities that would have helped Paul McCartney in his writing and singing.

Nadi Nakshatras

These are special nakshatras counted from your birth nakshatra – some good and others difficult. Avoid people with nakshatras that are difficult and embrace those who are friendly. Transits to these nakshatras can give experiences according to their nature.

Janma nakshatra – the 1ˢᵗ nakshatra, the same as at birth, is Ashlesha. If his parents, brothers, sisters, or children were born with the same nakshatra, McCartney would need to do remedial measures, but as I do not have their birth data it is not possible to check.

Karma nakshatra – the 10ᵗʰ nakshatra from Janma is Jyeshta. Transits to this nakshatra and people with this nakshatra would be helpful to him professionally and help him experience and create the right karma. McCartney became the first artist to sign with the Starbucks label 'Hear Music' on 21 March 2007 when Jupiter was transiting Jyeshta.

Sanghatika nakshatra – the 16ᵗʰ nakshatra from Janma is Shatabhishak. It can create wrong associations, and people with this nakshatra are to be avoided. Transits to this nakshatra could also bring the wrong type of people into his life.

Samudaya nakshatra – the 18ᵗʰ nakshatra from Janma, is an auspicious one. This is Uttara Bhadra for Paul.

Vinasha nakshatra – the 23ʳᵈ from Janma, is the most negative nakshatra. This is the Rohini nakshatra for Paul. Heather Mills' time of birth[3] is unknown and there is the possibility of her Moon being either in Rohini or Mrigasira. Considering the animosity this relationship generated, I feel this shows Heather's Moon to be in Rohini. The relationship would therefore have created negativity from the start. When you meet people with your Vinasha nakshatra, for no apparent reason enmity can develop. On a subliminal level, there can be aggression or hatred, which obviously leads to a difficult relationship. It may not bring destruction, as it will in extreme circumstances, but the McCartney/Mills relationship did not appear to be a happy one and their divorce has been very acrimonious.

Manasa nakshatra – the 25ᵗʰ from Janma. Ardra is the 25ᵗʰ nakshatra and gives added information about the subtle mind. Ardra is connected to the intellect and its ability to both create and destroy and McCartney's amazing output as a composer of music and lyrics has show the great

---

3. Heather Mills, born 12 January 1968, Aldershot, UK. Time of birth unknown.

mental powers that he has. He has also changed (destroyed) one aspect of his career to move onto another one several times.

Gandanta or Difficult Nakshatras
His moon is not in Gandanta.

Nakshatra for Prayers
Paul McCartney should give Ashlesha as his nakshatra when visiting a temple or doing puja.

5

TITHI

In *Varaha Purana*[1], Sage Mahatapas, a great ascetic, says that humans are all born from Hiranyagarbha, the universal womb. Every person represents a separate principle of creation, all being distinct yet the same, and each person is connected to the atma, the eternal soul that never dies. A portion of this eternal soul comes through the Hiranyagarbha to Earth in the form of the jiva atma, the living soul. The Sun is atma and the Moon is jiva atma. The daily distance between the Sun and Moon is a tithi. The principles of divinity are the deities that rule the tithis: Agni, Ashwini Kumaras, Gauri, Ganapati, Nagas, Kartikeya, Aditya, Matrs, Durga, Diks, Kubera, Vishnu, Yama, Rudra, Chandra and Pitris. Examining the tithi at the moment of birth will show what divine principle you are working with and how to deal with and get the best out of it.

Varaha Purana further adds that the imperishable Soma has sixteen digits. *Soma* is the Moon. The sixteen digits are the fifteen tithis and one moment of silence at the end of the 15th tithi. Soma is also the amrita, the nectar of immortality that we carry within our souls. The nectar is stored in a virtual pot between the ajna and the sahasrara chakras, and it is only when this pot of nectar overflows that humans find eternal happiness. The incarnating soul has collected this precious nectar by its good deeds in previous lifetimes, but human nature is such that it wants to use it all up through the urge to fulfill its desires. The Moon represents both the nectar of immortality and our ability to deplete it; the Vedas say we should preserve it. The vedic way of living with its many spiritual practices was specially designed to preserve this nectar and add to it. The pot of nectar is replenished with our good deeds, through dedicating our life to higher causes, living a good life and learning to control our desires.

---

1. Puranas are classical vedic texts that were written after the Vedas. They give many myths connected to vedic astrology and are a rich source of information. Varaha Purana details legends about the tithis that are used in this chapter.

The tithis represent the different natures of human life, which if properly understood give us the opportunity to preserve the precious amrita that the soul has gathered over its previous lifetimes. It shows our weaknesses and our strengths, our ability to relate to others as well as our connections to the deities. Each tithi is a personification of a deity that divided itself into two halves. One half remained in eternity while the other came down to Earth to face the law of karma and guard the soul.

The Tithi Basics

From their conjunction at the New Moon, the Sun and the Moon move away from each other at the rate of 12° per day. This is known as a lunar day or a tithi. A lunar month has thirty tithis. Each tithi is slightly shorter than the solar day and a lunar year is 48 weeks. Tithis are the lunar steps to and from the Sun, the daily interaction of the living with the eternal.

The lunar month is divided into two fortnights known as pakshas. The pakshas are:

1. Shukla paksha – the bright half of the Moon, from the New Moon to the Full Moon. 15 tithis belong to the waxing cycle of the Moon.
2. Krishna paksha – the dark half of the Moon, from the Full Moon to the New Moon. 15 tithis belong to the waning cycle of the Moon.

In the Indian almanac, the tithis are always represented by numbers from 1 (the first day) to 15 (the Full Moon). After the 15th day of the lunar cycle, the next tithi is known as number 1 again, then 2, 3, 4 and onwards to 14. The 30th day, the darkest night of the lunar month, is known as amavasya and number 30 represents this. The tithis of both the bright and dark half of the month are below:

Day	Tithi	Deity
1.	Pratipada	Agni
2.	Dwitiya	Ashwini Kumar, Brahma
3.	Tritiya	Gauri
4.	Chathurthi	Ganapati
5.	Panchami	Naga, Saraswati
6.	Shashti	Kartikeya

7.	Saptami	Sun
8.	Ashtami	Shiva, Krishna, Matrgana
9.	Navami	Durga
10.	Dashami	Yama, Diks
11.	Ekadashi	Vishwedeva, Kubera/Vayu
12.	Dwadashi	Vishnu
13.	Trayodashi	Kamadeva, Dharma
14.	Chaturdashi	Shiva, Rudra
15.	Purnima	Soma
30.	Amavasya	Pitris

Purnima tithi is the Full Moon and amavasya is the dark Moon. The start of purnima is 12° before Full Moon, and it is at the end of purnima that the Full Moon is total. Immediately after that is krishna pratipada, the 1st day of the waning Moon. Amavasya begins when the Moon is 12° away from the Sun. Amavasya is often referred to as the New Moon as at the end of the tithi the New Moon rises and shukla pratipada, the first day of the waxing cycle, begins.

Tithi Degrees from the Sun

No	Name	Shukla	Krishna
1.	Pratipada	00°00 to 12°00	180°00 to 192°00
2.	Dwitiya	12°00 to 24°00	192°00 to 204°00
3.	Tritiya	24°00 to 36°00	204°00 to 216°00
4.	Chathurthi	36°00 to 48°00	216°00 to 228°00
5.	Panchami	48°00 to 60°00	228°00 to 240°00
6.	Shashti	60°00 to 72°00	240°00 to 252°00
7.	Saptami	72°00 to 84°00	252°00 to 264°00
8.	Ashtami	84°00 to 96°00	264°00 to 276°00
9.	Navami	96°00 to 108°00	276°00 to 288°00
10.	Dashami	108°00 to 120°00	288°00 to 300°00
11.	Ekadashi	120°00 to 132°00	300°00 to 312°00
12.	Dwadashi	132°00 to 144°00	312°00 to 324°00
13.	Trayodashi	144°00 to 166°00	324°00 to 336°00
14.	Chaturdashi	166°00 to 178°00	336°00 to 348°00
15.	Purnima	178°00 to 180°00	
30.	Amavasya		348°00 to 00°00

Tithi Bhuta
The main tithi bhuta is Apas, the water element. Tithi shows our emotional stability and happiness. The water element makes this important for relationships, love and how we deal with individuals, as Venus is the primary ruler of the tithi. The strength or weakness of Venus in the natal chart would add or detract from the quality of the tithi. A tithi can also show compatibility – often people of same tithi get on well together. Each tithi also has its own bhuta ruler as well.

Five Sets of Tithis and their Sub-bhutas
There is a sub classification of tithis, which is linked to the panchamahabhuta. Tithis are divided into sets of five that repeat themselves over six times, thrice in the waxing phase and thrice in the waning. In this classification each set of three tithis are known as nanda, bhadra, jaya, rikta and poorna. Nanda tithi are 1, 6, 11 tithis; Bhadra are 2, 7, 12 tithis; Jaya are 3, 8, 13; Rikta are 4, 9, 14, and Poorna are 5, 10, 15 or 30 tithis.

Type	Tithi	Bhuta
Nanda	1,6,11	Agni
Bhadra	2,7,12	Prithvi
Jaya	3,8,13	Aakash
Rikta	4,9,14	Apas
Poorna	5,10,15	Vayu

Nanda reflects the agni bhuta, bhadra reflects prithvi, jaya: aakash, rikta: apas, and poorna: vayu. We must study how the sub-bhuta of these tithi classifications relates to the water element of the tithi. The relationship between the two elements decides how you will deal with emotions, love and personal relationships.

Of these the rikta and nanda tithis can have problems with relationships. Rikta – because they need relationships too much, and nanda – because they are too fiery and this can dry up their emotional sensitivity.

Rikta means unsupported and individuals born in rikta tithis can feel insecure and unloved; they feel the lack of support acutely. Apas bhuta is emotional and needy but rikta further aggravates this; the more they seek it, the greater the instability. As both the tithi and the rikta bhuta is apas, the double water energy can create overpowering emotions, yet water gives no support to itself. It is the rikta tithis that feel the need for relationship most, but they may remain unfulfilled as their emotional needs never get the proper sustenance. They could seek blessings from the deity that rules the rikta tithis as a remedy: 4 tithi – Ganesha, 9 tithi – Durga, and 14 tithi – Shiva. The remedies are given in Chapter 8.

The fire sub-element of the nanda tithis conflicts with the water element of the tithi. Agni heats the water (emotions) up and can then dry them completely. Persons born in nanda can become so extremely passionate, they may be too much for others to handle, or their emotions can become burnt up so there is nothing left to give. As a result their relationships/emotions quickly get out of control and there is lack of balance – too much or too little. This makes them hard to understand and not always easy to love. Regarding relationships, the following is often true:

Apas tithi (rikta) are good at relationships but as they are rikta tithis, their inner insecurities can create problems for them. They need partners who support them as their emotional neediness is at times too much for others to manage.

Prithvi tithis (bhadra) sustain relationships. They want relationships that last.

Vayu tithis (poorna) can easily churn up their emotions. They need steadiness from relationships or else worry and stress can cause them problems.

Agni tithis (nanda) burn up relationships and are the worst offenders for selfish and short-term relationships.

Aakash tithis (jaya) protect relationships.

Tithi Pravesh – Tithi birthday
Originally birth dates were always given in terms of tithis rather than calendar dates of birth. When I asked my grandmother her date of birth, she told me that she was born at sunrise on the 5th tithi of the month of bhadra (Sun in Virgo) in the year George V visited India (1911).

Birthdays are traditionally celebrated on the day of the solar return but as this only takes into account the position of the Sun, it does not give the complete picture of the coming year.

The annual birthday can be celebrated in two more ways as well. One is on the day that the Sun is in its birth rashi and the Moon is in the birth nakshatra. If the Sun at birth is in Leo and the Moon in Ashwini, the annual birthday will be the date when these two are in their natal positions but not necessarily their degrees. This is known as the nakshatra birthday.

The second is tithi pravesh. *Pravesh* means to enter. The day the tithi is the same as on the day of birth – in effect the angle between the Sun and the Moon is the same this day is taken as the annual birthday. The Sun must be in the same sign as the birthday and the tithi must also be the same: this shows different degrees for both the Sun and Moon. If the Sun is in Leo and the tithi is shukla panchami, then annual shukla panchami when the Sun is in Leo is celebrated as the tithi birthday and the chart studied to see what the year has in store.

You have monthly nakshatra birthdays and tithi pravesh too: first is the monthly lunar return and second is the monthly tithi return. The monthly tithi return takes place when the tithi is the same as at birth – here it is not essential for the Sun or Moon to be in the same nakshatra. The annual return when the Sun is also in the birth sign is given the greatest importance. In temples, priests will do special prayers for individuals for these monthly nakshatra and tithi returns. If the birth day is with Sun in Aries, Moon in Rohini and shukla tritiya (3rd) tithi, then the monthly return of the Moon in Rohini is as important as the shukla tritiya. Both will be regarded as mini birthdays but the main celebration would be in the month when the Sun also gets back to Aries.

The birthdays of vedic deities are always celebrated monthly on the tithi returns and their annual celebrations take place on the tithi pravesh. The vedic god, Shri Krishna was born with the Sun in Leo, Rohini nakshatra and krishna ashtami (8th day) at midnight. His monthly birthday is celebrated on ashtami whereas the major celebration called janma ashtami takes place annually when the Sun is in Leo and ashtami tithi. Ashtami tithi annually may not always be in Rohini nakshatra.

Individuals should study this chart for their yearly analysis but also use this day to celebrate their birthdays. The solar return chart shows only the Sun's exact position. The nakshatra return shows the exact

Moon's quality. It is the tithi chart that shows how the Sun and Moon relate to each other annually and this is why the yearly chart analysis should be made from tithi pravesh along with the solar return chart. Also for a finer analysis, the monthly nakshatra and tithi return charts need to be studied. Tithis pravesh, along with the monthly nakshatra and tithi returns give a new picture of the annual chart and reveal a deeper understanding of how the year unfolds.

Bill Gates was born on shukla trayodashi on 28 October 1955. His Sun is in Libra and his Moon in Uttara Bhadra. His solar return for 2007 would be when the Sun returns to the same degree as his birth Sun – 11°45' Libra, which would be around 28 October 2007. Whereas the tithi pravesh birthday will be anytime between 17 October and 16 November – when the Sun is in Libra – then on shukla trayodashi, his tithi birthday will be celebrated. This is 24 October 2007, 11 November 2008, 31 October 2009 and so on. His annual nakshatra return would be on 24 October 2007, 10 November 2008, 30 October 2009. There can be differences between the tithi and nakshatra return. Bill Gates' monthly nakshatra birthday will be when the Moon returns to Uttara Bhadra and the monthly tithi is shukla trayodashi, not the krishna one. Positive or negative planets on these monthly tithis or nakshatras will modify the quality of the tithi pravesh chart.

The importance of looking at the annual chart this way is that it can give a different degree for the Sun and a different nakshatra for the Moon annually and shows the true picture of the year.

Shraddha and Tithi of the Day of Death
Shraddha means faith and reverence. In this context it means reverence to the pitris, the forefathers or departed souls (parents, grandparents and others), and is one of the important duties of every person according to Hindu belief.

Shraddha are performed in the krishna paksha (waning Moon fortnight) before the New Moon in Virgo. The fifteen tithis from krishna pratipada to amavasya when the Sun is in Virgo is dedicated to remembering the dead. The rituals performed during this time give great religious merit, ancestors are worshipped and every effort is made to satisfy their wishes so they can rest in peace for the remainder of the year. This fortnight is known as pitru paksha.

For shraddha ceremonies it is important to know the tithi of the death date of your ancestor. Even if your ancestors died on a shukla paksha, you only consider the tithi. The corresponding tithi of krishna paksha becomes important annually during the shraddha, so if your ancestor died on shukla saptami, you will do their shraddha on the saptami of the pitru paksha. Favourite food items of the departed person are specially prepared and offered after performing a puja, donations are given and people travel to Gaya or other spiritual places to give special offerings. A small portion of the food is also offered to the wild crows. The Crow is considered a connection between the living and dead worlds.

The shraddha performed during pitru paksha are not funeral ceremonies, they are rather pitru-yagya, or worship of the ancestors as deities. This is different from the worship of the gods. Shraddha is mainly performed for three generations of pitris, namely the father, the grandfather and the great grandfather. When performed for all the ancestors, seven generations of ancestors are believed to benefit from it.

The final day of pitru paksha is the mahalay amavasya. This starts when the Moon is 12° away from the Sun in Virgo. All the ancestors are prayed to at this time and the belief is that they come down to Earth from their abode and join the world of the living for a day.

The Dagdha Rashis, the Burnt Signs

Each tithi has certain rashis that get burnt and so become disfunctional. These are known as *dagdha rashis* (burnt signs). We don't know how or why they get burnt but this is the law regarding the tithis. Dagdha rashis are mentioned in *Muhurtha Chintamani*. Dagdha rasi is also known as shunya rashi. Shunya means quiet, zero, without any energy. The dagdha rashis in different tithis are:

	Tithi	**Dagdha Rashis**
1.	Pratipada	Libra, Capricorn
2.	Dwitiya	Sagittarius, Pisces
3.	Tritiya	Leo, Capricorn
4.	Chathurthi	Taurus, Aquarius
5.	Panchami	Gemini, Virgo
6.	Shashti	Aries, Leo
7.	Saptami	Cancer, Sagittarius
8.	Ashtami	Gemini, Virgo

9.	Navami	Leo, Scorpio
10.	Dashami	Leo, Scorpio
11.	Ekadashi	Libra, Capricorn
12.	Dwadashi	Aries, Libra
13.	Trayodashi	Taurus, Leo
14.	Chaturdashi	Pisces, Gemini, Virgo, Sagittarius
15.	Purnima	none
30.	Amavasya	none

The dagdha rashi creates problems for the houses it rules, and the planets that are placed in them. The rulers of the dagdha rashi become negative wherever they are placed.

When analysing the effect of the dagdha rashi ruler by conjunction, it is important to study its effect on the karaka of the planet it is placed with. If the dagdha lord is Jupiter and is placed with Venus (the karaka for relationships and wife), the individual may have problems in that area. If Venus were the dagdha ruler, then its placement with Jupiter would create problems in having children and regarding the husband in female charts. There are certain modifications to this rule:

- Retrograde planets placed in the dagdha rashis flourish.
- If these rashis are aspected by Jupiter, they tend to lose some of their negativity.
- Rahu Ketu prosper in dagdha rashis as they only travel retrograde. Usually malefics (malefics by nature or due to rulership of dusthana houses) fare better than benefics.
- If avayogi is burnt, that is good as it is a negative planet and it loses the capacity to cause harm. (More on avayogi in Chapter 7).
- When the same planet rules two houses, only the house that is dagdha suffers.
- A negative house being dagdha is better than a positive one.
- Dagdha lord placed in Rahu Ketu nakshatras does well.

During their dashas, the ruler of the dagdha rashi and the planets placed in the dagdha rashi can fail to give their full results. In my opinion the dagdha rashi shows underlying weaknesses or the inability to get full profit from these issues, but it does not spoil everything.

If the birth takes place on panchami, the dagdha rashi would be Gemini and Virgo, but the houses that become dagdha depend on the ascendant. If the ascendant is Scorpio, then the 8th house and the 11th house are Gemini and Virgo respectively. The 8th house is dusthana, a negative house and, according to the modification rule on dagdha rashis, a dagdha rasi ruling a negative house is not so troublesome. In this case the quality of the 8th house improves, though there may still be issues of inheritance. It does not mean a lack of inheritance but the pleasure you receive from it is diminished, there may be emotional problems connected with finances. The 8th is the money house of partners, so there may be obstacles that are not immediately visible. Finally the 8th is the speech of partners, and this may be burnt, bitter and not very sweet. The 11th is the house of profit. Being dagdha it does create issues around not feeling that you earn enough or that you are unable to enjoy your earnings. Usually there is a mental block about earning/profit; it is not the amount you earn but how you feel about it. Also 11th house is the elder sibling; expect strained relationships, lack of joy in the family ties, or some problems that you cannot fully understand through other astrological analysis. Do take care in using these factors independently without doing the full analysis of the chart.

Tithi Gandanta

The last 48 minutes of poorna tithis and the first 48 minutes of nanda tithis are called Gandanta. Gandanta is a spiritual knot which needs to be unravelled before the soul can move on.

Poorna tithis are the 5th, 10th and 15th or 30th tithi and the nanda tithis are 1st, 6th and 11th tithis. This can be a difficult time of birth as there are subtle blocks that stop life from progressing in the right way. It is important to get remedial measure done for these birth times. Remedial measures are explained in Chapter 8.

Birth on the Lunar Pakshas
Shukla paksha – the waxing Moon

The bright half of the moon gives a naturally outgoing personality. Shukla paksha people like to meet others, their mind is inquisitive, they are searching for answers from this world. They enjoy life and usually revel in good relationships and are open, friendly and generally have a good disposition.

Krishna paksha – the waning Moon

Krishna paksha people are more private. They internalise their emotions and find them difficult to express, so the issues their personalities throw up cannot easily be discussed. They will be happy in meditative moods but they have to learn to say what they feel. They nurture secret passions, are restless, quick to anger, and more fickle than their shukla counterparts.

Tithi Personality

Being born in a tithi gives certain qualities to the personality. The deity of the tithi is important as the person is supposed to be the living essence of this god. The good qualities of the deity, as well as their struggles, become personality patterns in the humans.

Pratipada. The first steps of the Moon away from the Sun (shukla) or towards the Sun (krishna) belong to Agni. From the stirring of the great cosmos arose Agni, the great fire. A fire of a thousand flames is also said to rise from the anger of Narayana (Vishnu). Fire brings offerings from the gods to the humans; a divine energy hungry for gratification. Narayana tells Agni he will feel gratified by taking the offerings for the gods and offerings to Agni (in the form of food) are given during prayer ceremonies held daily in temples and homes of devotees. But the true offerings to Agni are given by those who live a life dedicated to God without care of outcome and who offer their physical body good food as prasadam (God's food). They also submit their skills to the divine and take their pleasures as an aspect of divine creation. They feed their inner soul with spiritual intentions, which can lead to moksha, self-realisation. But if they constantly feed the wrong foods of ego, ambition, self love and selfish desires, the fire gets bigger and bigger, gobbling up all it is fed, wanting more and more. The desires get out of control and the soul remains forever thirsty; the path of moksha obscured.

The soul born on pratipada has a tall order to fill, but must recognise the fire principle that the more it is fed, the bigger it gets. The immense energy generated can bring destructive elements like anger and aggression, but if these people use the energy wisely and keep their inner fire under control, it brings purity, divinity and the right path to higher knowledge. Anger can be a weakness for pratipada and so can over-ambition and never-ending needs and passions.

Pratipada people are usually scholarly, wise, wealthy, honoured, visionary, fiery, ambitious, successful and innovative. They can also be angry, aggressive, autocratic and dominating. Those born in shukla pratipada (post New Moon) are more dynamic and adventurous, looking to fulfill desires and hungry for success. Those born in krishna pratipada (post Full Moon) are calmer personalities, more stable and comfortable in their vision. Their desires may be better fulfilled.

Dwitiya. The second step away from the Sun (shukla) and the second step towards the Sun (krishna) belong to Ashwini Kumaras. Ashwini Kumaras, the twin sons of the Sun god, are physicians to the gods. Beneficent and with great curative powers, they had the ability to restore youthfulness and rejuvenate the old. They represent the duality of life in the connection between heaven and earth, day and night, past and future.

Ashwin means a cavalier or a horse tamer. Horses represent our senses, desires and creative energy, and a cavalier's ability to tame horses is connected to the ability to master cravings. Ashwini Kumar in dwitiya can bring the desires that are unleashed by Agni in pratipada under control. Ashwini Kumara personify prana and apana. Prana is the life force and also the in-breath. With every breath we take, we energise the body with spiritual energy. Apana is the out-breath and with every out-breath we release the toxins of the mind. Understanding and regulating the in and out breaths allows us to control the agitation of the mind and to control wayward desires. Yogis and adepts will practice pranayama in order to control their mind, instincts and desires. This allows them to aspire to preserve their soma (amrita) rather then spend it.

Dwitiya know about control. They may struggle with duality, trying to be everything to everyone. They are morning people, natural healers, forever youthful, good at yoga, and sporty. Generous, virtuous, happy, wise, popular, able to control their desires, kind, truthful, excellent workers, good with horses...these are their positive traits. Negative qualities would include their opposing natures, and their tendency to be controlling, dominating, unstable and overcome by their needs. The shukla dwitiya searches to learn control and mastery of their desires, whereas the krishna is more disciplined with their desires.

Tritiya. The third step away from the Sun (shukla) and the third step towards the Sun (krishna) belongs to Gauri. Gauri is the wife of Shiva and is also known as Parvati, Sati, Uma, Ambika... to cite just a few of her other names. Gauri means the fair one and Gauri personifies speech, with its power to heal and wound. Cruel words can hurt immensely and leave an indelible mark on the psyche whereas uplifting and spiritual words give calmness and blessing. Speech is how we connect with others.

Tritiya celebrates the goddess or the feminine principle that supports the male. Tritiya was the day Gauri married Shiva; it is connected to the union of opposing forces. Gauri is a role model for the perfect wife, she has a connection to the ideal husband (Shiva) and a marriage that lasts forever. Gauri has many incarnations and in each one she marries Shiva. The need for relationships, to find divine love and commitment is a Tritiya impulse. These people will make many sacrifices for love but can be too idealistic in their search, ignoring relationships that appear less than perfect or sacrificing too much for unworthy partners. They are clever, sensuous, proud, passionate, scholarly, spiritual, nurturing, and good speakers. They can have addictive personalities – to the opposite sex, to their sensual nature, following fasts in their effort to control them. They often live away from the place of birth. The shukla tritiya people are more fickle and unable to settle down, ever searching for love, whereas the krishna will want to settle down and be with a partner. All the tritiya people need relationships in their life. If the Moon is afflicted they may have a propensity to use their speech in a negative, sharp way.

Chathurthi. The fourth step away from the Sun (shukla) and the fourth step towards the Sun (krishna) belongs to Ganapati. Ganapati is the son of Shiva and Gauri. Ganapati is also known as Ganesha, Vinayaka, Vighneshwara etc. Ganapati was born of the four great elements, earth, water, fire and air. He represents the fifth element aakash that protects the people. According to one of the myths of his creation, Shiva created him with his laughter. He was a beautiful boy, shining and luminous in the sky, just like Shiva, but when Gauri saw him she forgot about Shiva and Shiva was so angry with his wife for ignoring him that he cursed this glorious child to have a face like an elephant, a protruding belly and a belt of snakes. His anger also created many ganas in the image of

Ganapati, who fell to Earth. *Gana* means multitude, the public, the followers, and each gana was accomplished and bright. The ganas began disturbing the balance on Earth so the gods requested Brahma to control them. Brahma asked Shiva to make the elephant-headed boy Ganapati, the leader of the ganas. Ganapati is very bright and clears all obstacles from the path of those who pray to him.

Chathurthi people are natural leaders and protectors of others, clearing obstacles for them. If they want their own obstacles cleared, they need to seek the blessings of Ganesha, then whatever obstructs them can be removed. They can make life very easy for themselves as they develop the knack of overcoming hurdles. They are courageous, adept with words, argumentative, intelligent, adventurous, fierce, Machiavellian, risk takers, orators, legal brains, writers and gossips; and may often feel unsupported. The shukla chathurthi people are able to break through obstacles, whereas the krishna need to ask for divine blessings and may feel more obstructed in life.

Panchami. The fifth step away from the Sun and the fifth towards the Sun belongs to the nagas. Nagas are serpents, originally poisonous, violent and deadly. Humans begged Brahma to save them from these terrible serpents that were killing them with their venom and he promised protection. Brahma cursed the serpents and told them they would face a serious decline, but the serpents fell at his feet and begged 'Oh Brahma, you created us wicked, how can you complain that we follow the path we were created for. Please reduce our venom and give us a separate abode from the humans'. Brahma relented and gave them the underworld (Patala, Vitala and Sutala) and a boon that if they bite those who trouble them they would not be punished, although humans could kill those who were insolent and fierce. The nagas came to symbolise all that is secret and hidden, the possessors of great occult powers. They carry their poison in a pouch; their body is not filled with poison and they use it only when forced to do so. The nagas have the capacity for both good and bad; the poison can be used for healing or for killing. If we take the story of the nagas as a parable that poison exists within all of us, the moment we learn to recognise these poisons we are able to live with them without making our life toxic. Panchami people have a great ability to control and overcome their sins.

Panchami represents the primary struggle of man between his good and evil nature. Panchami can express either emotion within the individual. These people can be overly attached to their negative sides as they think this is their nature and it is how they will go on living. But recognising their negative disposition allows them to change, to accept it and not necessarily use it. They can be very fierce if cornered or if they feel in danger and may live in their own world, hidden and private from others. Panchami can lead people to knowledge, secret wisdom, wealth and prosperity, but it can also take them down the path of danger, self-destruction, sexual adventure and wrong uses of the occult. If they understand themselves and their role in this world they will be generous, compassionate, lucky, respected, ascetic, stable and sincere, with the ability to control their senses. They can have good relationships and many friends. Their negative qualities are viciousness, jealousy, possessiveness, secret agendas and anger.

Shashti. The sixth step away from the Sun and the sixth step towards the Sun belongs to Kartikeya. Kartikeya is another name for Mars. A Kartikeya is born in every yuga when people need help to fight the demonic forces. Each birth of Kartikeya takes place to defeat the demons. The myth of his first birth tells us that the gods needed a commander for their forces that were being annihilated by the demons and they went to Brahma who asked Shiva to have a son who could take up such a mantle. Shiva excited his body and from that excitement rose Kartikeya, glowing like fire. The origin of Kartikeya is told differently in different yugas. (Read the story about his second birth in Krittika nakshatra). Kartikeya became the commander and illuminated the world with his radiance. He is the source of strength and valour who leads his forces to victory.

He personifies the ahamkara (ego) that controls all our actions and desires. Usually these people can be extremely egotistical, thinking they are the best and all they do is of their own making. Shashti people have to learn to restrain their ego and surrender to the divine forces. As the commander, Shashti was born to fight the demons, and this illustrates the symbolic fight with our inner demons: the ego, the lack of acceptance of divine will. Shashti people are bright and powerful with the ability to lead. They can fight for the right causes and will be courageous. Usually they keep their word, and are vigorous, passionate, athletic, energetic, popular, intelligent, and aspire to fame. But they can also be arrogant, domineering, controlling, aggressive, and easily injured. They are great friends to have in times of trouble as they will protect and fight for your cause but they can refuse to accept authority. This leads to achievement but also to absolute power. They can do foolhardy things as they are unable to listen to wise counsel; in effect they only learn from their own mistakes. They enjoy the opposite sex but are not always good with relationships and intimacy, they can become obsessed with them and allow these emotions to rule them.

Saptami. Seven steps away from the Sun and seven steps towards the Sun belongs to the Sun itself. When the eternal soul wanted to personify itself it came as light encompassing all the lustre of knowledge and all the radiance of eternity, in order to illuminate the three worlds. It was called by many names, Aditya, Surya, Bhaskara, Savitur, Prabhakara, Ravi, Divakara etc. From this splendour came the twelve suns, one of which the world revolves around. It protects the world but can destroy it as well. The gods, the sages, the siddhas and humans all prayed to the Sun god and accordingly he only showed its gentle, warming side to them. While Surya has the capacity to burn and destroy, those who understand its power and honour its energy will only feel its positive glow. The Sun's radiance falls on all and sundry, but not all understand the true role of the Sun in our life as they are dazzled by the outer brilliance and forget to look for the Inner Light.

The Sun can restrain desires. Saptami burns up human desires so that they are no more. When eternal knowledge dawns, the soul can control or burn up its desires, but if the knowledge is blocked, the soul keeps on feeding the desires until they get bigger and bigger, with no end in sight. The positive aspect of Saptami is the mastery of desires leading to fulfillment, while the negative aspect is the inability to do so and feel only frustration. Most of the Saptami-born hover between the two – some desires they can easily master while others they struggle with. They are caught between fulfillment and frustration. Saptami people aspire for the knowledge of Brahma, they respect spirituality, honour God and can be visionary thinkers and philosophers. They are warm, with good leadership qualities; discerning, ambitious and focused on what they want to achieve while appreciating the good deeds of others. An inability to fulfill their overwhelming desires can make them feel frustrated and angry. Arrogance, imperiousness, and being overpowering and dominating can be some of the negative features. Surya usually has many wives and therefore a lack of commitment to one relationship is possible.

Ashtami. Eight steps away from the Sun or eight steps towards the Sun belong to the Matrikas, the divine mothers. Andhaka, a demon, was terrorising the world. When Shiva in the form of Rudra tried to kill him, from each drop of Andhaka's blood rose another demon. Even Vishnu, Kartikeya and Indra all joined the fight but it appeared impossible to win. Then Shiva's anger created the goddess Yogeshwari, and the other gods followed, manifesting seven more goddesses: Vaishnavi from Vishnu, Brahmi from Brahma, Kumari from Kartikeya, Mahendri from Indra, Yami from Yama, Varahi from Varaha and Maheshwari from Narayana.

Goddesses always represent the shakti (power) of the gods. Each brought her own shakti.

Goddess	Created by	Shakti
Yogeshwari	Shiva (Rudra)	love
Maheshwari	Narayana	anger
Vaishnavi	Vishnu	greed
Brahmi	Brahma	pride
Kumari	Kartikeya	ego
Mahendri	Indra	rivalry
Yami	Yama	bitterness, spite
Varahi	Varaha	tolerance

These forms of the goddesses show the weaknesses of man but also his ability to restrain them. The goddesses sucked the negative blood from Andhaka and he lost all his malignancy and became a powerful adept. The ability of Andhaka's droplets of blood to regenerate shows how our weaknesses can multiply if unchecked, till they obscure everything in our life. This tithi celebrates female power. While tritiya celebrates women, ashtami venerates their power and their ability to remove fear and conflict.

Ashtami can reflect all the human frailties and the inborn

capability to overcome them if we try. It is possible for the Ashtami-born to go from weakness to strength, to become good, spiritual and strong and be truly happy, prosperous, wealthy, caring, educated people, loving and being loved. But if these people do not change their life can be overshadowed by restlessness, greed, anger, pride, arrogance, competitiveness, possessiveness, bitterness, intolerance and a lack of peace of mind. Not everyone will have all these weaknesses but they may struggle with one or two of the above.

Navami. This is nine steps away from the Sun and nine towards the Sun and belongs to Durga. Durga is a female power and has the ability to overcome the demons that terrorise the world. Durga personifies maya, the world of illusion we live in. Durga fought the demon Vrtrasura for a thousand years and killed him single handedly, saving the three worlds of body, mind and spirit. Whenever we talk of the demons we must relate them to the inner demons that the soul fights in its journey for enlightenment and liberation from unhappiness and pain. Durga fighting the demon Vrtrasura for a thousand years indicates that this is not an easy fight. We struggle with our inner demons for a long time but we should not give up. Durga is extolled as Saraswati, the giver of knowledge, as Mahamaya the great illusion and as the mother goddess. She is the prana, the bhutas, justice, good fortune, speech, the holy cow, the eternal and the great intellect. She helps people break free from their sorrows and removes their demonic energies.

Usually navami people feel oppressed with their inner demons and feel unsupported. They need to fight for a long time to overcome their inner anxieties, fears and worries as they can be attached to their world of illusions. They tend to relate to the temporal world, which is maya, and that is the root cause of their anxieties. But they also have the power to control this world around them, fighting whatever negative comes their way. They must believe in themselves. Navami people can be musical and love dancing; they are courageous, strong, powerful and committed to their cause. Endurance to fight the fight is their specialty, but they can also be opposed and aggressive to others and feel unsupported and insecure. This insecurity leads to negative conduct; and a tendency to become fierce, angry and agitated.

Dashami. This is ten steps away from the Sun and ten steps towards the Sun and belongs to the Drigs, the female virgins. The Drigs were created from the ears of Brahma as he wanted someone to be able to protect and hold all that he had created. They were radiant, beautiful, virginal, pure and dignified, and Brahma also gave them husbands. One Drig he married himself and gave the others nine husbands who became the drigpalas, the guardians of the ten directions. The ten directions are the four primary directions (east, west, north, south) zenith and nadir (upward and downward) and the four half directions (northeast, southeast, northwest and southwest). East is where the sun rises, west where it sets, north and south where it travels towards during the day. The protectors of the world are the husbands of these ten virgins. They are the aristocrats, royalty who were meant to guard human creation. Each of the directions has a virginal deity and husbands who represent certain qualities.

Directions and their Drigs

Directions	Drigs	Drigpala	Power
Upward	Udharva	Brahma	supreme power
Downward	Andharva	Ananta Naga	boundlessness
East	Purva	Indra	power
South East	Shraddha	Agni	devotion
South	Dakshina	Yama	justice
South West	Niritti	Niritta	misery
West	Pratici	Varuna	knowledge
North West	Bhadra	Vayu/ Kubera	wealth
North	Uttara	Soma	wealth, amrita
North East	Sati	Isana	purity

The essence of dashami is to guard what is created and to support others who are creating. There is not much conflict here except to be supportive and hold on to what is there. It is a very good tithi to be born under as these people will be pure, wealthy, intelligent, wise, temperate, passionate, liberal, courteous, protective, creative and humble, with leadership qualities and a keen grasp of the scriptures. Even if they go the wrong way, it is usually because they want to protect others; they get worried and unsettled if they do not have anything to protect. They can also be ambitious but feel useless if they do not have major projects to nurture. They should remember that protecting what is close to them is just as important.

Ekadashi. The eleventh step away from the Sun and the eleventh step closer to the Sun belongs to Kubera. Kubera is the god of wealth and the manifestation of the great element Vayu, the wind. Vayu arose out of the mouth of Brahma. Vayu was blowing hard, disturbing the peace and showering hailstones, but Brahma calmed it down by giving it a job to do, and made it the guardian of wealth, Kubera. Kubera is also known as Dhanapati, the preserver of wealth. It indicates that when the individual gets to preserve what they create they make even more of it as their energy gets used properly. Otherwise they can become agitated and revel in destructive behaviour.

Ekadashi shows the ability to utilise energy in the right way. These people can convert the destructive into the constructive. Vayu deals with communication, mobility, travelling, and the sense of touch. The Ekadashi-born will be good communicators. They cannot be controlled but they can learn to harness their energy for great wealth and prosperity. They are natural at making money and creating serious wealth. These are artistic, multi-skilled people, happy, godly, pious, puritan, focused, honest, wealthy, good in business and saving reserves, and following the dharmic path. On the negative side, if they waste their energy or do not know how to make the best use of it, they can be destructive, overly focused on making money, wasteful and unsettled.

Dwadashi. This is twelve steps away from the Sun and twelve steps towards the Sun and belongs to Vishnu. As a god, it is difficult to take on material tasks so Vishnu decided to embody himself so that he could do his duties. He represents the mind and its embracing ability to create, preserve and destroy. This is a good tithi to be born under as Vishnu is the preserver of all aspects of creation. He came to destroy ignorance with the help of his sword and with the Sudarshana chakra he severs the unfavorable influences of the wheel of time. With a mace he destroys unrighteous behaviour. He annihilated the sins accumulated from different lifetimes and with the help of Vayu, gave success over illusions. The Sun and Moon guide his vision, and the goddess Laxmi is by his side. He has formidable weapons to make his tasks easier.

Those born in dwadashi have many ways and skills for protecting their creativity; special qualities that set them apart from others. Their minds are bright and strong and they are practical, charitable, honoured, well-behaved, mercurial and knowledgeable; willing to follow the right path and fight ignorance, poverty, and social injustice. Laxmi the goddess of wealth is always with them and can indicate good relationships as well as being lucky in wealth creation. Their negative traits can be over confidence, laziness and restlessness. There is some tendency towards destructiveness, which can be troublesome.

Trayodashi. This is thirteen steps away from the Sun and thirteen steps towards the Sun and belongs to Yama. The Moon in the krishna trayodashi is getting weaker and more hidden so krishna trayodashi people are private, ascetic and more apt to be loners than their shukla counterparts. Yama is the god of death and represents dharma, righteous behaviour. He is also known as Dharma or Dharmaraj, the king of dharma. Dharma has four padas or feet, which signify truth, purity, penance and charity. They also stand for the gunas (quality), dravya (sustenance), kriya (action) and jati (caste, creed, genus). Yama protects the world with four padas in satya yuga, three padas in tretya yuga; two in dvarapa yuga and only one pada in kaliyuga. We are now living in kaliyuga and there is very little support from dharma. Without dharma both gods and demons behave badly for dharma means living in a good way and following the right path. The Moon does not like dharma, as it does not want to be disciplined. It fought with Dharma over his love for Tara, Jupiter's wife, and Dharma got ostracised. But this created a major war between the gods and the demons and the world was slowly slipping into chaos. So Brahma restored Dharma from his exile and again Dharma set the rules. All levels of manifestation in the different worlds, the gods, demons and humans, are said to benefit from the rules of dharma. The Vedas believe that without a dharmic way of life even our good qualities (gods) do not behave, and the bad ones (demons) behave even worse.

The trayodashi-born are fond of discipline and following the right path. This can make them too restricted by rules and conditions and not always ready to have fun for fun's sake. Those who want to enjoy life or lead a less than perfect life cannot understand trayodashi and can in some cases be inimical towards them. But following conservative behaviour, rigid rules, and the right path regardless of the cost to oneself, is what makes trayodashi who they are. They can be clever and virtuous, good at setting policy agendas and undertaking religious fasts, and they make knowledgeable though strict teachers and good politicians, but can have conflicts with family and friends over behaviour. They are not usually beautiful or at least they do not feel attractive. They can be boring and not much fun if they become too rigid in their ideas and perpetually opposed to those enjoying life. Morality campaigners would be a good representation of trayodashi.

Chaturdashi. Fourteen steps away from the Sun and fourteen steps closer to the Sun belongs to Rudra. The krishna Moon is getting dim, its light is weak. Rudra is a form of Shiva. Rudra means the crying one. Because Brahma could not originally create the world in the way he wanted, his frustrations and anger manifested as Rudra, a divine entity who cried incessantly. Lord Brahma tried to stop him from crying and said *Tvam Ma Rud*, which means you don't cry, and this is how Rudra got his name. Brahma wanted Rudra to commence creation, but since Rudra lacked the power needed for creation, he had to develop these skills through penance in the spiritual oceans. In the meanwhile Brahma created Daksha Prajapati from his mind and Prajapati helped him in the creating of the universe.

Rudra's penance was disturbed by the constant chanting of the mantras at the yagya performed by Daksha Prajapati to which both gods and demons were invited. Rudra became infuriated that he wasn't invited and the creative process had begun without him and his anger obstructed the yagya and the devas lost their ability to perform the rituals. Brahma asked Rudra to calm down and asked the devas to pray to Rudra so that he would give them their knowledge back. As the devas praised the great Rudra as Shiva, Mahadeva, Shambhu and Visvesvara, Rudra became pacified and asked the gods what he could do for them. The gods asked Rudra to give them the knowledge and secrets of the vedas, shastras and yagyas. Rudra agreed to give them this knowledge as long as they accepted him as their god. The gods agreed and achieved moksha from it.

Chaturdashi is not an easy tithi to be born under. As a rikta tithi, people can feel unsupported. Rudra's impact shows that lots of tears and sacrifices are needed if you want to learn wisdom and secret knowledge.

Krishna chaturdashi have to pay a heavier price than the shukla. They want respect, and just as the other gods did not originally respect Rudra, this is a respect that has to be fought for. Although Shiva has an ideal wife, his relationships have not been easy and chaturdashi people can inherit these issues. Anger can be a great weakness but they are witty, funny, greatly skilled, and have easy mastery over a number of subjects. They have mental and physical prowess, are good at yoga, have a strong constitution and are helpful to friends and relatives. They have to be careful that their humour does not become spiteful as they can also be cruel or intolerant, aggressive and emotional. For children born in krishna chathurthi, there are remedial measures to be performed when they are young to take the sting out of this tithi. If you were born in this tithi and the remedial measures have not yet been performed, you should read about the remedies in Chapter 8 and try to do them now.

Purnima. This is fifteen steps away from the Sun and belongs to Soma, the Moon god. Soma was married to the twenty-seven daughters of Daksha Prajapati, a myth of the nakshatras we have explored in *The Essentials of Vedic Astrology*. His favourite wife was Rohini. Daksha asked him to treat his other wives equally but Soma refused so Daksha cursed him and Soma disappeared into the ocean. Gods, men, beasts and plants all began to wither in the absence of Soma. The gods pleaded to Vishnu to restore their beloved Soma so Vishnu called Rudra, Brahma and Vasuki and together with the gods and demons they churned the ocean and Soma reappeared. His visible form is the jiva atma, the living soul within the body. He took on the sixteen digits that form the tithis and it is his sixteenth digit that sustains the gods while the fifteen other faces help the living world. Water is his manifestation and Shiva wears him in his hair.

At purnima, the mind is fully bright and the emotions are calm. The living soul feels truly connected with the eternal one. These people do not always follow the dictates of others easily even if it costs them dearly and they may easily attract the wrath of the establishment, but they do have an abundance of everything. They can be rich, happy, lucky, satisfied, charming sensual, pleasure-seeking, with many relationships, and a special connection with herbs and plants. They are essentially good people and when in love they are willing to sacrifice everything for it.

Amavasya. This is when the Moon is on the last step to the Sun on the night before the New Moon. It is the darkest night of the month and belongs to pitris. Pitris are forefathers and this is the day that is celebrated for the dead, the past. Pitris guide humanity and manifest through the sense organs. Although they usually remain hidden, pitris protect humanity and when their advice is sought they will guide us in the right direction. As they represent the tanmatras, the subtle forms of matter, they went to Brahma eager to ascend into the sky to do penance. Brahma asked them to become the forefathers or ancestors of the human beings.

Amavasya is a difficult birth day; the issues are subtle. There is a strong awareness of senses and desires, the need to express underlying emotions, but not always with success. As both the karanas (more in Chapter 6) under amavasya are negative, there is little relief. It is important to study the nakshatras, the dina and the yoga before making a final conclusion. It is easy for these people to lose their direction and they need to follow a spiritual path to allow themselves to be in control of their senses rather than being under their influence. They can be very emotional, unable to control their desires, secretive, private, easily distressed and devoted to the parents. They have a weak constitution, are wanderers who love travelling, and earn with great effort.

Tithi Analysis

Princess Diana was born on chathurthi, which is a rikta tithi. This would have made her emotionally very needy and lacking a sense of security. The two burnt rashis are Taurus and Aquarius. Taurus rules her 7th house and Venus, its ruler, is placed in it. The question most often asked about her chart is how did she have such bad experiences with relationships when she had the 7th house ruler in the 7th house creating a Malavya yoga? But when you understand that the 7th house is burnt and its ruler, by being placed in the 7th house, is also affected, you can see her relationship issues more clearly.

The other dagdha house is the 4th, that of home, family and happiness, and the Moon and Ketu are placed there. Ketu as a retrograde planet flourishes in dagdha houses whereas the Moon feels totally bitter and unhappy. Ketu is not well placed in the 4th but with more force here it can be a greater negative influence. Diana suffered from rejection from her mother at a young age when her parents divorced, and then had a very difficult relationship with her step-mother. Also the lord of dagdha

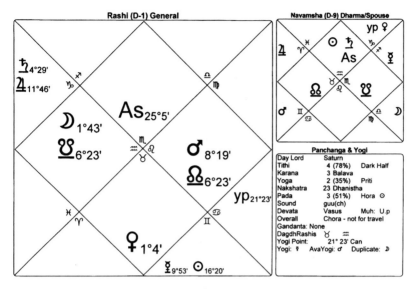

Princess Diana
1 July 1961, 19.25. Sandringham, England
Birth Tithi – Krishna Chathurthi
Dagdha Rashi –Taurus and Aquarius
Death Tithi – Krishna Chaturdashi

Aquarius, Saturn, is in the 3rd house with Jupiter, the karaka for husbands. This further caused problems for her regarding relationships. Not only is Jupiter debilitated, it is being adversely influenced by Saturn, the dagdha lord. Her marriage to Prince Charles was very unhappy but she also died with Dodi, who was her current partner. Also Saturn in the 3rd house showed a strained relationship with her younger brother.

Her tithi paints a very sad picture for Diana. This is a unique chart with lots of problems and others may not suffer to similar extremes. It is important to do remedial measures but sadly it is too late for the Princess.

She was pronounced dead on 31 August 1997 at 3am, Paris, France on krishna chaturdashi. Her sons, Princes William and Harry, should honour her memory annually by doing shraddha on krishna chaturdashi when the Sun is in Virgo; this will allow her soul to rest in peace. The tenth death anniversary shraddha day for Princess Diana would have been on 9 October 2007. In 2008, it would be on 28th September and in 2009 on 17th September. The Princes William and Harry celebrated their mother's tenth death anniversary on 1 July 2007 – on krishna pratipada.

6

KARANA

The Karana is half a tithi. Karana is derived from the word *Kar* whose meaning is to do. *Karana* means doing, performing, producing and creating. It represents the karma we create in this lifetime.

Karana Bhuta is Prithvi
Karana reflects the prithvi bhuta, the practical side of man, and it is important in creating new karma. The karanas have the ability to strengthen or spoil a tithi. As the tithi has apas bhuta, karana's prithvi is important for support. Karana represents the underlying influences, so if there is no karana support, apas can feel very insecure. Karana has to be studied as an important subordinate to the tithis and not the other way around.

Karana Chakra is Muladhara
Muladhara is the base chakra that supports the incarnation. For incarnating souls it is essential to have a strong support to life so they can aspire to greater things. If they feel unsupported it can make things tougher. Being born on one of the difficult karanas can take this reinforcement away, so it is essential to do remedial measures to help build a sense of being strongly earthed.

Tithi Basics
A karana is the 6° difference between the Sun and the Moon, and there are sixty of them. There are thirty tithis and sixty karanas: eleven types of karanas: four fixed and seven movable.

The fixed karanas are shakuni, chatuspada, naga and kintughna. All are complex karanas to be born under and do not offer much support to their tithis. The four fixed karanas start with the second half of the 14th day of the krishna paksha, amavasya, and the first half of the 1st tithi of the shukla paksha. The first karana in shukla paksha is always the fixed kintughna. Fixed karanas do not repeat themselves and are always ruled by Rahu or Ketu, showing past life issues and fixed karma that needs to be atoned for now. If children are born on any of the fixed karanas, parents should perform remedial measures.

The seven movable karanas are bava, balava, kaulava, taitila, gara, vanija and vishti. They start with bava on the second half of the first tithi and repeat themselves in the same order eight times in a lunar month. Each movable karana has the same rulership as the dina starting from the Sun and ending in Saturn. Of these vishti is a difficult karana and can spoil the tithi it appears with. Vishti karana occurs in the following tithis: In shukla paksha it covers the second half of chathurthi, the first half of ashtami, the second half of ekadashi, the first half of purnima; and in krishna paksha it covers the second half of tritiya, the first half of saptami, the second half of dashami and first half of chaturdashi.

Karanas of the Shukla Paksha – the Waxing Moon phase

Tithi	First Half	Planet	Second Half	Planet
1.	Kintughna	Ketu	Bava	Sun
2.	Balava	Moon	Kaulava	Mars
3.	Taitila	Mercury	Gara	Jupiter
4.	Vanija	Venus	Vishti	Saturn
5.	Bava	Sun	Balava	Moon
6.	Kaulava	Mars	Taitila	Mercury
7.	Gara	Jupiter	Vanija	Venus
8.	Vishti	Saturn	Bava	Sun
9.	Balava	Moon	Kaulava	Mars
10.	Taitila	Mercury	Gara	Jupiter
11.	Vanija	Venus	Vishti	Saturn
12.	Bava	Sun	Balava	Moon
13.	Kaulava	Mars	Taitila	Mercury
14.	Gara	Jupiter	Vanija	Venus
15.	Vishti	Saturn	Bava	Sun

Karanas of the Krishna Paksha – the Waning Moon phase

Tithi	First Half	Planet	Second Half	Planet
1.	Balava	Moon	Kaulava	Mars
2.	Taitila	Mercury	Gara	Jupiter

3.	Vanija	Venus	Vishti	Saturn
4.	Bava	Sun	Balava	Moon
5.	Kaulava	Mars	Taitila	Mercury
6.	Gara	Jupiter	Vanija	Venus
7.	Vishti	Saturn	Bava	Sun
8.	Balava	Moon	Kaulava	Mars
9.	Taitila	Mercury	Gara	Jupiter
10.	Vanija	Venus	Vishti	Saturn
11.	Bava	Sun	Balava	Moon
12.	Kaulava	Mars	Taitila	Mercury
13.	Gara	Jupiter	Vanija	Venus
14.	Vishti	Saturn	Shakuni	Rahu
30.	Chatuspada	Ketu	Naga	Rahu

Krishna chaturdashi and amavasya are the two most difficult tithis to be born under as both their karana are difficult. They therefore feel a total lack of support from their karana and its earthly (prithvi) qualities.

Karana Personality

Bava means strong. It is ruled by the Sun and aspires to success and power. These people will be good leaders, wealthy, scholarly, musical and passionate. A weak or poorly placed Sun can bring a lack of confidence, arrogance, poor leadership qualities and a perpetual need for support.

Balava means stronger. The Moon rules it so 'stronger' here represents a strong mind. A clear good mind is essential to achieve success as the mind will not then block karma that has to be achieved. These people will travel at lot and their aim is to be successful and strong. They are clear thinkers, strong minded, powerful, brave, pleasure loving, sensuous, poetic and artistic. They can be popular and involved in many relationships but if the Moon is placed negatively in their chart, it can lead to duplicity and deception.

Kaulava means of a noble family. Mars rules it and Mars wants to achieve success regardless of any hurdles. These people feel they belong to the aristocracy and will try to be at the top of their profession. They will protect, guard and make others feel safe, but can be selfish themselves.

They will be adventurous, good, free thinking, popular, well spoken and sensual, but a weak Mars can see them separated from their family and they may waste their energies and due to their lack of ambition they may be low achievers.

Taitila means a rhinoceros. Mercury rules it so these people will be intellectually bright and worldly wise. As the karana bhuta is prithvi and so is Mercury's, they will be practical, good at business and very committed to work. They are godly, wise, sporty and skilled in the art of sexuality, but can be stubborn, unsteady, aggressive and restless. A weak Mercury can make them confused, changeable and untrustworthy.

Gara means swallowing and destroying poison by antidote. Jupiter rules it and these people are judicious, patient, good advisors, liberal and physically well proportioned. They have control of their negative traits and show special skills in dealing with poisons: actual and those of the mind. A weak Jupiter can make them money minded, conservative and negative.

Vanija means trader or businessman. Venus rules it so these people would have an eye for beauty, and appreciate art and music. Finances can be another speciality. Whatever they do displays an artistic touch and they are creative, cheerful, knowledgeable, honourable, and good advisors who earn through trade and business. A weak Venus can make them depressive and lack artistry; they may be too critical and strive too hard for perfection.

Vishti means poisonous. It can promote dubious qualities making the individual prone to their weaknesses. Saturn rules it and usually vishti karana people are dealing with poisons from a past life. These people can be possessive, jealous, bitter and angry, which influences the way they act or react to situations. It does not block them from being successful but there is always a residual bitterness within them. It is important to pray to Shiva to destroy these poisons so they don't influence the karma being created. Vishti will also create added negative karma that will need to be dealt with in the future – the position of Saturn in the birth chart shows how you deal with this. If Saturn is retrograde, combust, debilitated or without aspect of Jupiter and Venus, then the poisons of Vishti will be much in evidence. The problem is not with poisons but how you deal with them. An extremely negative vishti promotes bitterness, anger, laziness, tamas and viciousness, whereas a good vishti indicates the control of anger, the ability to deal with poisons, bravery, competitiveness, hard work, and democratic behaviour. Vishti people can be very successful in their chosen fields but can always feel they did not achieve what they set out to; somehow others rob them of their due success. Remember this is in the mind; the reality may be quite different. The strength or weakness of Saturn in the natal chart has a lot to say about how vishti will behave.

Shakuni was the uncle of Duryodhana in the Mahabharata and assisted him in many crooked schemes. Shakuni is also someone (especially an old relative) whose schemes and projects lead to failure and ruin, or someone who preys on the helpless. This is obviously not a good karana to be born under. Shakuni is ruled by Rahu who can represent the lowest of the low in the materialistic world, but Rahu also has the ability to transcend towards the highest of the high if it focuses on the spiritual[1]. By understanding the weakness of Rahu one can rise above it and become wise and profound. It takes lots of effort. A strong Rahu would help, and good aspects of Jupiter and Venus would keep the negativity down. Shakuni can give a doubting, suspicious, and skeptical mind. These people can be expert in mantras and the science of omens but although they have a good temperament their suspicious nature may spoil things. Prosperous and eccentric, they are always waiting for omens to manifest before they commit themselves to anything, and must be careful that wrong advice does not take them down a ruinous path. I feel shakuni will experience loss due to wrong advice or decisions. They must also learn to trust as their nature is overtly suspicious.

Chatuspada means four-footed or animal-like. Ketu rules it. There are past life issues to deal with and these people can be very internalized and mystical with an interest in deep spiritual science. They are not always good at using these talents commercially and are often short of money

---

1.   More on Rahu in *The Lunar Nodes - Crisis and Redemption*.

and funds due to their lack of concern about financial matters. They do have a way with animals and can be good vets or farmers but they also have a base nature, which they must try to develop into a higher one. They are not physically strong, enjoy crude jokes and can be very earthy and sensual.

Naga means snake or serpent. Rahu rules it. Naga can be very profound or totally vicious and quarrelsome, so these people must learn to control their more negative tendencies. Naga have the deep wisdom of snakes and often change their life through painful experiences. They can be private and secretive and are good warriors, developing patience and fortitude when fighting for causes. They can achieve great success but must always try to curb their more extreme, obsessive behaviour.

Kintughna means a possibility, something not fully formed; an aspiration. It also means a spider or a worm. Ketu rules it. Ketu brings forth past karma that is not fully developed at present and Kintughna can develop the potential either way depending on the strength of Ketu and the lagna lord. Their ideas may seem eccentric, they may not be interested in money, but these people can be successful if they trust their instincts and work in innovative areas of life. Otherwise they can have a deep connection with past life secrets and make it their life's work to bring them to public attention. What they need is a vocation, not an ordinary job. They can be sexy, passionate and have many relationships. They regard all as equal and will not bow to unnecessary shows of wealth or strength, and they are atheists and will not care for religion.

From the krishna chaturdashi to shukla pratipada, the fixed karanas make the qualities of these tithis more negative. The weaknesses of those born under these tithis are highlighted and their struggles become harder. Vishti and shakuni are the underlying karana for krishna chaturdashi; these can bring Rudra's extreme qualities to the fore and many tears are shed in trying to gain what they think is rightfully theirs. Vishti can increase bitterness and negative behaviour while shakuni can make them suspicious of everyone's motives. Suspecting others does not make for good relationships and they have to learn to calm themselves down.

Chatuspada and naga fall in amavasya. Amavasya is a tricky time to be born, with subtle energies bubbling away and many negative qualities that a soul can embrace if it is not careful. Kintungha is in pratipada and comes under the guidance of agni. It can certainly bring out the more aggressive qualities of agni.

Parashara suggests remedial measures for vishti, krishna chaturdashi (vishti and shakuni) and amavasya (chatuspada and naga). Read about them in Chapter 8.

Professions and Karanas
Karana shows how you go about your work. The karakas and qualities of the planetary ruler of the birth karana shows inherited talents and the aptitude for certain professions. Even difficult karanas can be talented in areas of life. The Mars, Saturn, Rahu and Ketu professions can be enhanced if these planets are either placed with Jupiter or Venus or aspected by them. Similarly good karanas can be spoilt and the wrong profession taken if the influence is of Saturn, Rahu, Ketu or Mars.

To truly understand the profession of an individual we also need to study the 10th house, its rulers, atmakaraka, and the divisional charts: navamsha and dasamsha.

Professions represented by **Bava** (Sun): Doctors, healers, stockbrokers, leaders, commanders, politicians, industrialists, heads of state, civil servants and forestry workers.

Professions represented by **Balava** (Moon): Politicians and those who are elected by public mandate, farmers, travellers, sailors, fishermen, journalists, healers, doctors, nurses, counselors, carers, and trade connected with alcohol, tourism, advertising, shipping, the Navy, exports and imports. Balava supports all careers where popularity is the key ingredient and it can give easy celebrity status in the chosen profession.

Professions represented by **Kaulava** (Mars): Police, military, mining, geology, engineering, computers, mathematics and all technical disciplines, leaders, commanders, surgeons, warriors, logicians, estate agents, property dealers, sportsmen, athletes, firemen, dictators and yogis. Kaulava people can be great ascetics as Mars has the courage to control all desires and give up the material way of life. Usually these people will have a different career first and are then able to sacrifice it. Kaulava's main instinct is to protect and defend those who come under its guardianship.

Professions represented by **Taitila** (Mercury): All types of business, traders, accountants, writers, journalists, publishers, teachers, intellectuals, astrologers, entertainers, authors; the media, telecommunications, internet, television; and often two professions.

Professions represented by **Gara** (Jupiter): Spiritual teachers, gurus, lawyers, judges, scholars, professors, priests, stockbrokers, voluntary workers, charity workers, philosophers, serious authors, publishers, ministers, advisors; plus jobs which have respectability attached to them like deans of colleges or universities, leaders of inquiry commissions etc.

Professions of **Vanija** (Venus): Artists, actors, musicians, fashion designers, perfumers, businessmen, traders, car dealers; jobs connected with movies and theatre, the luxury goods sector, jewellery and its allied trades, plus treasury jobs from finance minister to income tax officers,

Professions indicated by **Vishti** (Saturn): Judges, magistrates, ascetics, teachers, researchers, builders, masons, surveyors, the service industry, the iron and steel industries, the department of justice, the gambling industry; plus servants, labourers, and all low paid and unsettled jobs that require long hours and hard effort.

Professions indicated by **Naga** and **Shakuni** (Rahu): Politicians, astrologers, pilots, dealer of poisons, doctors (if Rahu has an aspect to Jupiter), gamblers, spin doctors, spies, advisors (but they have to watch what advice they give), those who work in unconventional jobs, and those who work with reptiles especially snakes.

Professions indicated by **Kintughna** and **Chatuspada** (Ketu): Ascetics, sadhus, astrologers, mystics, clairvoyants, past life specialists, researchers, militants, military personnel, farmers, vets, and any job that works with animals.

House Placement of the Karana Lord in the Natal chart

The house position of the karana lord gives added clues to the career of the individual. If your karana is gara, which Jupiter rules, you will study Jupiter's house position in the natal chart. Jupiter in the 1st house would show that the career is extremely important and that personality is essential to it. In **Whitney Houston's** chart[2], she has gara karana with Jupiter placed in the 2nd house of voice and inheritance. She was born with an amazing voice and is known internationally as a singer.

Karana Analysis

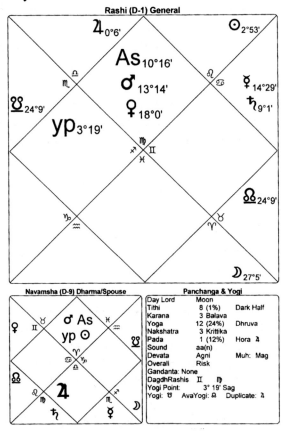

Bill Clinton. 8.41am, 18 August 1946, Hope, AR, USA.
Ashtami tithi and balava karana

2.   Whitney Houston, Date of birth: 9 August 1963, 20.55, Newark, NJ.

Ashtami tithi appears to be that of the politician. Tony Blair, George Bush and John Major are some of the politicians born on ashtami.

Bill Clinton's karana is balava, which is ruled by the Moon. The Moon in Bill Clinton's natal chart is placed in the 8th house and in Kemadruma yoga. The Moon at 29° Aries is almost exalted and it is in Gajakesari yoga with Jupiter. This shows a powerful mind, clear thinking, and other positive characteristics of balava. But Bill Clinton can also express weaknesses of the balava karana: multiple relationships, negative thinking and an unsettled personality. According to the myth, the Moon was cursed and the establishment ostracised him and Bill Clinton, a popularly elected leader and favourite with most Americans, had to suffer the humiliation of impeachment during his second term. The 8th house placement of the planetary lord of the karana can show unexpected scandals or transformations in career, though it gives political skills. His dina lord and atma karaka are also the Moon, further enforcing the qualities of his karana lord.

7

NITYA YOGA

Nitya means daily and *yoga* means a yoke or connection. The panchanga yoga is different to the yogas created by the planets as it is formed by the daily angle between the Sun and Moon. The Moon travels 13°20 away from the Sun each day and these 13°20 sections (similar in length to a nakshatra) form the Nitya yoga, a subtle blending of solar and lunar energies that give special daily indications. Aakash is the bhuta of the yoga, indicating what protection and blessing the individual has. There are 27 such yogas and each one is linked to a particular nakshatra. Some are malefic in nature and others benefic. The Nitya yoga at the time of the birth:

- Influences the personality

- Creates yogi and avayogi grahas – special planets that are positive or negative forces in the chart.

- Creates duplicate yogi – a second planet that is extremely positive and supportive

- Gives a secret point of prosperity and luck known as the yogi point.

Nitya yoga is the essence of panchanga. It can make or mar the quality of the panchanga as it deals with security, support and the feeling of beneficence. If the Nitya yoga does not give support, we feel bereft. A good Nitya yoga can eliminate the difficulties of the tithi and karana as well.

Nitya Yoga Basics
There are three methods to calculate the yoga:

1. Yoga = (Moon's longitude + Sun's longitude) / 13°20

2. Total the number of the Sun's nakshatra with the number of the Moon's nakshatra and subtract 1. The remaining number is the

number of the relevant nakshatra. If the Sun is in Ardra nakshatra, which is the 6th nakshatra, and the Moon is in Mula nakshatra, which is the 19th Nakshatra, then 6 +19 = 25 – 1= 24. The yoga of the day is number 24, which is Shukla, a good yoga.

3.   The method most popularly used is to take the longitude of the Sun plus the longitude of the Moon and add 93°20 (the longitude of the beginning of Pushya nakshatra).

All vedic software will calculate the Nitya yoga for you.

The Nitya Yogas

There are two types of yogas: good yogas and difficult yogas. The difficult yogas are Vishkumbha, Atiganda, Shoola, Ganda, Vyaghata, Vajra, Parigha and Vaidhrati. They usually show a lack of support, and these people need to make their own luck, whereas the good yogas (the remainder) tend to get help easily, feel blessed and protected. My experience is that the difficult yogas do not indicate a lack of success, neither do the easy yogas mean a lack of failure. It is the attitude towards them that makes the difference. Difficult yogas can make a person feel deprived, poor and unsupported even when they have all the material blessings in the world. Whereas easy yogas have an amazing ability to help people cope even when going through a dark period; they still feel blessed and supported. For the difficult yogas it is important to look inward and think of the blessings instead of always seeing the negativity; you can also do the appropriate remedial measures. The 27 Nitya Yogas are:

1.   Vishkumbha
2.   Preeti
3.   Ayushmana
4.   Saubhagya
5.   Shobhana
6.   Atiganda
7.   Sukarma
8.   Dhriti
9.   Shoola
10.   Ganda
11.   Vriddhi

12. Dhruva
13. Vyaghata
14. Harshana
15. Vajra
16. Siddhi
17. Vyatipata
18. Variyana
19. Parigha
20. Shiva
21. Siddha
22. Sadhya
23. Shubha
24. Shukla
25. Brahma
26. Indra
27. Vaidhrati

Nitya Yoga Bhuta is Aakash

Aakash is the bhuta of the yoga so it indicates what kind of protection and blessing the individual has, and whether they feel protected and supported in life.

Jupiter rules aakash and its position in the chart will further indicate how the Nitya yoga evolves. A weak or badly placed Jupiter in the natal chart can make even a good yoga difficult to handle whereas a strong Jupiter can help one cope with the difficult yogas in a constructive way.

The Chakra is Vishuddhi

Vishuddhi chakra has the ability to purify poisons. *Vi* means poison and *Shuddhi* is to purify. Vishuddhi chakra purifies the toxins within the subtle body and its connection to the Nitya yoga adds to its protective nature further. Nitya yoga helps protect the individual and even if they have issues raised in their panchanga or in the natal chart, a good Nitya yoga will give them skills to deal with it successfully. If the Nitya yoga is difficult the individual feels insecure and unprotected as they are unable to deal with life's challenges.

Yogi and Avayogi Grahas, Yogi Degree and Duplicate Yogi

Yogi graha is a planet for prosperity and avayogi graha can give bad luck or deprivation. Yogi and avayogi planets are usually connected to success or the lack of it; the yogi planet gives success, and avayogi denies it. The type of success, material or spiritual, depends on what you seek.

The exact degree of the Nitya yoga becomes the yogi point. The ruler of the nakshatra in which this point is found is the yogi planet, and the ruler of the rashi of the yogi nakshatra is the duplicate yogi. The yogi and the duplicate yogi are there to protect, bringing blessings, good luck and success in life.

The 6th nakshatra from the yogi nakshatra is the *avayogi* nakshatra and its ruler is the avayogi planet. Avayogi's role is to block blessings and make you struggle for success.

	The Yogas	Yoga Nakshatra	Yogi Planet	Avayogi
1.	Vishkumbha	Pushya	Saturn	Moon
2.	Preeti	Ashlesha	Mercury	Mars
3.	Ayushmana	Magha	Ketu	Rahu
4.	Saubhagya	P Phalguni	Venus	Jupiter
5.	Shobhana	U Phalguni	Sun	Saturn
6.	Atiganda	Hasta	Moon	Mercury
7.	Sukarma	Chitra	Mars	Ketu
8.	Dhriti	Swati	Rahu	Venus
9.	Shoola	Vishakha	Jupiter	Sun
10.	Ganda	Anuradha	Saturn	Moon
11.	Vriddhi	Jyeshta	Mercury	Mars
12.	Dhruva	Mula	Ketu	Rahu
13.	Vyaghata	P Ashadha	Venus	Jupiter
14.	Harshana	U Ashadha	Sun	Saturn
15.	Vajra	Shravana	Moon	Mercury
16.	Siddhi	Dhanishta	Mars	Ketu
17.	Vyatipata	Shatabhishak	Rahu	Venus
18.	Variyana	P Bhadra	Jupiter	Sun
19.	Parigha	U Bhadra	Saturn	Moon

20.	Shiva	Revati	Mercury	Mars
21.	Siddha	Ashwini	Ketu	Rahu
22.	Sadhya	Bharani	Venus	Jupiter
23.	Shubha	Krittika	Sun	Saturn
24.	Shukla	Rohini	Moon	Mercury
25.	Brahma	Mrigasira	Mars	Ketu
26.	Indra	Ardra	Rahu	Venus
27.	Vaidhrati	Punarvasu	Jupiter	Sun

The house where the yogi planet is placed in the chart becomes enhanced, whereas avayogi can cause trouble. The duplicate yogi is also a planet that helps. Thankfully, there is no duplicate avayogi.

The yogi point is an extremely positive degree in the natal chart. When benefics transit over this point you can expect major material success; the dashas of yogi planets give good results while avayogi will give negative.

If the natal lagna lord or any planet is placed exactly on the yogi point, it becomes specially enhanced. It is a great blessing to have lagna lord as a yogi planet. If the 9th or 10th lords are yogi planets, the individual achieves great success. If the lords are avayogi, then they can hinder. Planets placed on the exact degree of the yogi point become very energized and positive.

In relationship compatibility, if your partner's ascendant ruler is your yogi planet, it brings good fortune to the relationship, whereas if it is your avayogi planet, it can bring debt, pain and incompatibility. If you meet people whose lagna lord is your yogi planet, they will always be good for you. For example if your yogi planet is in Leo, then someone with a Leo lagna can be very good for you, and protective towards you.

The planets will first act out their roles in the natal chart. If the Sun rules the 8th house, and is placed in the 10th, it will first enact its role in bringing unexpected transformation into the career and an interest in 8th house issues; even long term health problems are possible but as a yogi planet it will also do good. Usually it is in the dasha of the yogi planet that it will express itself. The yogi planet brings protection and blessings, transformations lead to positive change and perhaps you get the right remedy for the health problem. The planet can bring both negative and positive results simultaneously according to its role in the natal chart and its position as the yogi planet. If the Sun is an avayogi and the ruler of the 8th house is in the 10th, it could create added problems in the Sun dasha.

It is important not to get carried away with the principle of yogi and avayogi planets but rather to view them as supplementary information that enhances the natal analysis. While they have the ability to alter the final judgement, they are not the only factor to consider.

Nitya Yoga personality

Vishkumbha means a jar of poison. Poison can be used as an antidote and for wrong purposes – it can make a person bitter so one has to be aware of this tendency and remember to keep the bitterness under control. If frustrations and bitterness are allowed to fester they will bring uncertainty. This yoga also gives wealth and the will to succeed, competitiveness, and happiness from spouse and family. These people like to travel and are very conscious of their physical beauty but can pay too much attention to outer looks rather than the inner person.

Preeti means the loved one. These yoga individuals are extremely attractive to the opposite sex, popular, spiritual, virtuous, eloquent, charismatic, resolute, good public speakers, easy to like, generous and happy.

Ayushmana means the famous or the respected one. These people work hard to succeed and earn wealth. They enjoy plants and gardens and will travel extensively. They are healthy but have the tendency to overeat. They are policy makers, interested in the judicial process, so can become good lawyers, judges, politicians etc.

Saubhagya means good luck. These people are generally lucky in all aspects of life. Things come easily to them and they do not have to struggle too much. They are talkative, speaking wise words, wealthy, earning through fair means, super intelligent, dharmic and have a keen sense of smell.

Shobhana means bright and shining and refers to a good intellect. These people are quick-witted, fast thinking and always have a ready answer to any question. Dignified, attractive, they like to do good deeds regularly and can think on their feet. They can be very sexual and passionate, appearing to be troubled by deep sorrow for no reason.

Atiganda means extremely knotted, a person whose soul energy is blocked. It is one of the most difficult yogas to have so I would recommend remedial measures. It promises neither success nor failure but the individual appears unhappy regardless of how successful they may be, however much money they may acquire. This can spoil the quality of their life and they must work hard spiritually to untie the knots of karma that are blocking the path of happiness. They are proud, strong, truthful and competitive in the extreme, charitable and brave – positive points which they should continuously emphasise. Their negative qualities can include a bad attitude to their mother, always blaming others for their problems, indulging in secret affairs and not feeling blessed even if from others' points of view they are.

Sukarma means good actions. These people are noble, wealthy, cheerful, artistic, generous, working for the good of others, good at business, courageous, confident, efficient and successful.

Dhriti means steadiness, constancy and in control of your life. These people are leaders, firm, supportive, constant, loyal, patient, and of good disposition. They may be attracted to perfumery. Their negative qualities include being fickle, lazy, greedy, prone to extra marital affairs and enjoying unwise romantic entanglements.

Shoola is a tough yoga to be born under. Shoola means pain, piercing, a sharp pointed weapon. Its malefic nature can make an individual aggressive despite what is promised in the birth chart. These people will be truthful, virtuous and of good character, but they can also be quarrelsome, angry, aggressive, and have an innate ability to hurt others emotionally. They can even be physically abusive if their natal chart accentuates it. They have to be conscious of their more negative tendencies and try to suppress them.

Ganda means a knot. It represents a karmic knot in the nature of the individual that needs spiritual understanding to unravel. It is not as difficult as the atiganda yoga, but it gives discontentment. It obstructs on the subtle psychological level and sometimes does not allow these people to develop spiritually. This yoga can spoil the nature and character if allowed to evolve. Hot temper, nastiness, deception and harshness are some of the negative traits that can develop. Material greed can be one of the spiritual knots ganda needs to unravel. Ganda yoga people are better off focusing on their positive forces like being friendly, talkative, truthful, serious, strong, eloquent and lucky. They must feel blessed by what they achieve rather than feel unhappy about what they don't.

Vriddhi means growing, increasing. These are generous, expansive people: intellectual, bright, brave, fearless, honest and chaste. They learn about trade and are good at business, loving to accumulate wealth. They are both sensuous and have the ability to control their senses.

Dhruva means eternal, everlasting, fixed and firm. These people are constant, unchangeable, strong, loyal, of good conduct, wealthy, learned, knowledgeable, and have the blessings of Laxmi (wealth) and of Saraswati (learning). Their weakness can be their inability to change.

Vyaghata means an impediment, a block, and it is a challenging yoga. These individuals are contradictory personalities, always going against trends. This can make them innovative and unusual but they will usually take the opposite view in arguments just for the sake of it, to be antagonistic. They are hard to understand, not always understanding themselves and must be careful not to become their own worst enemies, destroying what they love most. They can be achievers, strong in the face of any difficulty, forging their way through to what they have set their hearts on. Competitive by nature, they like nothing better than to fight for causes and get what they want, but they need to consciously temper their love for anger and violence. They can paradoxically be kind, helpful, brave and courageous, while also being dominating, aggressive and angry. They are respected for what they have achieved, but not always loved. The underlying weakness can set them back or stop their progress.

Harshana means happy, joyous. These people are cheerful, pleasant, love easily and are loved by all, popular, effervescent, they like farming, love the colour red, collect jewellery and ornaments and are scholars of classical texts. They are courageous and will destroy any competition. If they are deceptive and dishonorable it is usually in order to please someone.

Vajra means hard, severe, split. It is a weapon of Indra, like a thunderbolt. It can make people hard, uncaring, but also strong and fearsome. These people can fight any demon or negativity if they desire. There is a love of diamonds and they can acquire precision skills in cutting. They are intelligent, truthful, strong, brave, heroic, with many friends but their can also be severe and unfriendly. They will stand firm on their decisions, usually not taking into account others' views. They are passionate about what they like yet can be cold about what does not interest them. In relationships their hot and cold nature can confuse loved ones.

Siddhi means success, accomplishment, fulfillment of the object. It also suggests super human faculties that allow humans to overcome any obstacle. Siddhi is usually developed by those on a spiritual pathway to overcome their human frailty and become one with the divine. This is a great yoga to have. The ability to aspire for anything and achieve it can be on any level; for example an Olympian has Siddhi in his sport to give him/ her the ability to become super human in their pursuit of excellence. Good natured, religious, passionate, wealthy, speaking sparingly, liberal, philosophical, spiritual, studying Vedas and other classical texts, deeply knowledgeable metaphysically – these are some of their good qualities. It is also possible that they may use their power for the wrong reasons.

Vyatipata is a tough yoga to be born under. It means disrespect and deception and has the potential for an extremely difficult life event to occur that can scar the psyche. Usually parents will get remedial measures done for children with this yoga. There is a struggle for these people to keep their mind on spiritual things as they desire the material more. They listen to their parents and elders but are not able to respect them internally. They are truthful, caring, hardworking entrepreneurs with strong leadership qualities, but they can block themselves. They can be restless, unreliable, unstable and deceptive too.

Variyana means excellent, ambitious, and strong like a bull. These people will inherit money, be steady, loyal, committed, hardworking, careful in spending even when they are wealthy; they are also humble and have the ability to do boring work. They are very sexual and virile. Their weak points can be pride, stubbornness and boastfulness.

Parigha means a bar, a barrier or a hindrance. It also means a cloud crossing the Sun, indicating sudden shadows in an otherwise bright life. Again this malefic yoga shows the individual's potential to hinder or block themselves. These people are strong, powerful, compassionate, brave, generous and well spoken, able to achieve what they sent their mind to, yet their weakness of being economical with the truth and not caring about keeping good company, together with anger and aggression, can be their hindrance, stopping them benefiting from their good qualities.

Shiva means auspicious, propitious and lucky. Shiva is also one of the main gods of Hinduism whose role is to destroy ignorance. These people will remain happy, contented and successful. They know all about mantras and yantras, special skills in magic and spells, astrology and control over their senses. They are knowledgeable, calm, respected, honoured, chaste, pure and will make many pilgrimages. They are very conscious of maintaining a good public image.

Siddha means accomplished, attained, succeeded. It is also used for someone who is a divine being, pure and holy like a seer. This is an excellent yoga to be born under. The soul has aspirations for purity and a natural ability to be super human and rise above others. Being natural philosophers and thinkers, able to control their nature and override mere earthly conditions, makes them special humans able to succeed in what they set out to be. They are just, good at heart, expert in business, religious, multi-skilled and successful.

Sadhya means accomplished, good. It is sometimes also referred to as Satya, which means truthful and pure. Both the names for this yoga show the good qualities it endows. These people are humble, soft, faithful, loyal, intelligent, progressive, do well in business, sincere to their god/ guru, healthy, mantra shakti, gaining success by use of mantras.

Shubha means auspicious, radiant, and beautiful. Many superlatives in the same vein are given for Shubha. They will be lustrous, attractive, eminent, happy, virtuous, graceful, successful, wise, advisory, and achieve what they set out to be. They may suffer from a weak constitution.

Shukla means pure, white and bright. The mind is bright and pure. These people love the colour white. They will be skilled in debating and very keen to be successful and wealthy, competitive with a penchant for winning. They know how to control their passions and desires and are skilful in arts and music, but they may be too impulsive and talkative.

Brahma means wise, godly, religious, eternal. It is connected to the main Vedic god Brahma who is the creator. It gives the ability to be a creative ideas person, spiritual, scholarly and wise, enjoying the company of other wise men, and interested in the knowledge of Brahman (the eternal being). These people are resolute, strong, chivalrous, generous, dharmic, devoted to sacred knowledge and studious in connection with religious texts.

Indra means belonging to the senses, but here it also means the ability to master them. Indra is the god of gods and is a great warrior, a powerful personality who strives for victory especially over wayward desires and fights the demons to save the world. These people are gifted, famous, righteous, wealthy particularly from real estate, with a will to succeed and are popular and adored, treated like a king by friends and family. But they can suffer from kapha related diseases and may get involved in the wrong kind of relationships.

Vaidhrati is another malefic yoga. It means out of control, malignant, agitated. These people are fickle, fearful, nervous and unhappy, keeping the wrong kind of company. They lack reverence, are crafty and restless, and wealthy but not always from fair means. They often get blamed for other people's mistakes and this adds to their emotional burdens. They are hungry for success and therefore work hard to achieve it, but need to be careful they do not cut corners on their road to fame and fortune. They are usually successful, but their mind does not accept it.

Dealing with the Difficult Nitya Yogas
It is never easy to be born in a difficult yoga as it does affect the emotions of an individual. Those with complex yogas should make the effort to aim for higher things. Usually they may be atheists or do not believe in the pursuit of higher knowledge so they cannot always get help to resolve their inner conflicts. They must try to follow the path of truth as their insecurities can lead them into taking a wrong or unethical path, and they must learn to celebrate what they have achieved and not give in to dissatisfaction by comparing their life to those who they feel have achieved more. Doing remedial measures given in the next chapter would be a great help.

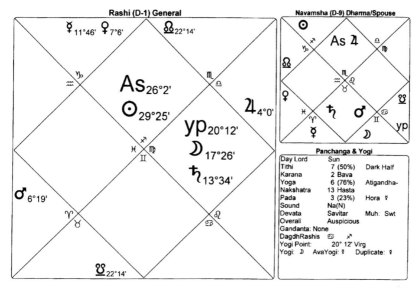

Rashi (D-1) General

‍ ♀ 11°46' ♀ 7°6' ☊ 22°14'

As 26°2'

☉ 29°25'

yp 20°12'

☽ 17°26'

♄ 13°34'

♂ 6°19'

♃ 4°0'

☊ 22°14'

Navamsha (D-9) Dharma/Spouse

☉

As ♃

Panchanga & Yogi

Day Lord	Sun	
Tithi	7 (50%)	Dark Half
Karana	2 Bava	
Yoga	6 (76%)	Atigandha-
Nakshatra	13 Hasta	
Pada	3 (23%)	Hora ♀
Sound	Na(N)	
Devata	Savitar	Muh: Swt
Overall	Auspicious	
Gandanta: None		
DagdhRashis	♋ ♐	
Yogi Point:	20° 12' Virg	
Yogi: ☽	AvaYogi: ♀	Duplicate: ♀

Swami Vivekananda
12 January 1863, 6.33am, Calcutta, India
Yoga is Atiganda
Yogi planet: Moon
Avayogi: Mercury
Duplicate yogi: Mercury

Nitya Yoga Analysis

Swami Vivekananda was a great spiritualist and philosopher credited
with bringing vedic philosophy to the West. He was also an inspiration
to the people of India during his short life through his many discourses
and countless books. Although he died in 1902, his many philosophical
works survive today. He was the main disciple of Ramakrishna
Parmahamsa and formed the Ramakrishna Mission and Ramakrishna
Math.

The reason I have chosen his chart is that he has one of the most
difficult Nitya yogas – Atiganda. Due to his spiritual and philosophical
life this yoga gave him the ability to develop the knowledge of the deeper
self and to untangle the knots of life. Usually a life of philosophy allows
an individual to dissolve negativity inherited at birth. Swami
Vivekananda's search for answers may have been guided by the insecurity
of the Atiganda yoga, but the path he chose allowed him to become a
powerful spiritual force instead.

The yogi planet is the Moon, which is placed in the 10th house very close to his yogi point at 20°12 Virgo. On 11th September 1893, the World Conference of Religions opened in Chicago, USA. Here his speech electrified the world. On this date Saturn was at 20°11 Virgo, exactly conjunct his yogi point. Saturn is not the best planet for his lagna, yet Saturn's role as the 2nd house lord of speech allowed him to give a most memorable address that inspired his audience and influenced western thought forever with his vedantic message.

Mercury is both the avayogi and the duplicate. Mercury loses its ability to do much harm as the avayogi is also the yogi; it fuses the success of the yogi with the denial powers of the avayogi, making it neutral – doing good and creating problems. Swami Vivekananda died in 1902 during a Jupiter Venus dasha. Mercury as the avayogi conjoins Venus and would have negatively influenced it.

8

PANCHANGA SHUDDHI – PURIFYING THE PANCHANGA

It is possible that the panchanga may be less than perfect – one or more limbs of the panchanga is difficult. For this reason parents should get the panchanga shuddhi done for the child. Shuddhi means purification and suggests that any dosha or weakness rising due to the panchanga can be improved and rectified. These remedial measures are essential in solving the issues raised by the panchanga.

Most of us who become aware of the panchanga at a later date and do not have the tradition of Jyotish in their chart can still learn to purify our panchanga. There is no need to remain in the darkness as these remedies do help.

Parashara points out that the main births for which panchanga shuddhi should be done is for those born on:

Gandanta – lagna, tithi and nakshatra
Krishna chaturdashi
Amavasya
Vishti karana

And birth in difficult yogas: Vishkumbha, Atiganda, Shoola, Ganda, Vyaghata, Vajra, Parigha and Vaidhrati.

The main tools of panchanga shuddhi are:

1. Yagya – worship and fire ceremony
2. Mantra and japa – reciting sacred sounds
3. Daan – donation; giving your time, support and money
4. Path of Yoga – mental, physical and spiritual clearing
5. Honouring the Sun and Moon gods
6. Honouring the gurus and brahmins
7. Feeding the poor
8. Seva and karma Yoga – looking after people and voluntary service
9. Following a dharmic path

You cannot purify the panchanga by wearing gems or colours of the planets.

Yagya – Offering

This is the most important aspect of the shuddhi. Yagya means offering, and life should be one long sacrifice to the higher energy. It is not sacrifice in the way the West may think, but more devoting your life towards a higher path and doing everything for the cause of it. This life does not expect rewards for actions done, but if rewards do come they are taken as a gift from God. This is the message of Bhagawad Geeta. It is a very high concept and those who can do their work without expectations find they get very high rewards for them, both material and spiritual.

There are two types of yagya. One is the offering made at temples or at home to the gods through fire rituals, the other is an inner yagya performed by an individual through meditation, chanting, japa, good dharmic acts, inner cleansing and learning to work selflessly for the good of the world.

The yagya is usually done by the priest through Agni, the fire god who is invoked to take the message from humans to the devas (gods). For panchanga shuddhi the yagya should usually be performed immediately after birth but it can be done at a later date. It is important to go to a local temple and ask the priest to perform this ceremony. Part of this yagya, an elaborate fire ceremony, is done where different types of offerings are given to Agni, with the chanting of the Vedas accompanying the ceremony. Donations are given to the priest and other priests are fed along with the guests. This yagya helps dissolve negative energies that are blocking the path of the individual in the subtle realms. But in my view, just doing the yagya is not enough, one must consider the purification practice through the inner yagya which can take a long time and helps a lot. Some of the inner yagya practices are given in the remedies below.

Mantra and Japa – Reciting Sacred Sounds

This is one of the most important element of the inner yagya. Mantras are sacred sounds or prayers that are addressed to a deity or planet, and repeating them continuously is japa. The sounds form an energy that burns away negativity from the subtle body.

Man also means the mind or thoughts and *tra* means to protect, so the mantra literally protects the mind through chanting sacred hymns.

Mantras did not originally have any meaning. They were single words like Om or Ram, Lam, Vam etc. The mantra has to reach the place to which it is directed. If you are praying to the deity, you focus the mantra towards that; if you are unhappy, you ask to be made happy while chanting; if you are creating light and purifying your panchanga, you must focus specifically on that.

Mantras are powerful but everything depends on how you chant them; they are recited in different ways. Sometimes the vowels are stretched so they can reach where they are meant to go. Sometimes mantras have just one word or a series of words. The importance and power of the mantra lies in its vibration. The vibrations of the mantras reach different parts of the physical and subtle body and beyond. As thousands of mantras have been chanted since time immemorial, we also connect to this when we begin chanting.

Mantras repeated constantly become japa. Japa is used to cleanse the mental and higher planes. You can also do japa by writing the mantras down in a notebook 108 or 1008 times. This becomes a meditative exercise.

Mantras are either effective or ineffective. Their weakness or strength depends on how they are chanted, pronounced and with what degree of faith. If done properly it is called a strong mantra. If not, then it is weak and may not be potent.

Usually a mantra is chanted either once, thrice, 28 times or 108 times. Once should be enough but if you decide you need to do more, you try for 108 times, which is the ideal number. Sometimes people decide they are going to perform 10,008 or 100,008 mantras over a particular period in order to show their devotion to the deity. In my opinion, if you do it right with the correct attitude, the mantra will be effective performed just once daily, but it should be done regularly.

Japa can be done in greater numbers – 108 or 1008 daily. This is extremely helpful with any of the difficult panchangas.

Mantras for Panchanga Shuddhi
Remember you must only chant mantras if you have faith in them. Listening to a recording of these mantras does not count as recitation.

One must learn to do them oneself, and the mantras must be recited in Sanskrit; translations do not have the same effect. Mantra vibrations resound on the subtle areas of the mind and can be good to break negative blocks.

Short Mantras

Short mantras are excellent for japa as they are easy to repeat and they resound in the outer realms and help clear the energy. The best short mantras are given below.

> Om
> Om Gam Ganeshaya Namah
> Om Namah Shivaya
> Om Namo Narayanaya

Long Mantras

There are three important maha mantras. Maha mantras can be chanted by all and have no negativity attached to them.

Gayatri Mantra

> Om Bhur Bhuva Svah
> Tat Savitur Vareneyam
> Bhargo devasya dhimahi
> Dhiyo yo na prachodayat

The meaning of this mantra is that we pray to one who exists for all time; on Earth (bhur), in the atmosphere (bhuvah) and in heaven (Svah). We mediate upon the glorious Sun in the form of Savita. May he illuminate our intellect and point us to the right path.

Gayatri means 'the mantra when chanted saves the singer' and is described in the Vedas as a mantra that helps us find divinity within. This is the highest of all mantras. Gayatri mantra is a prayer to the spiritual Sun and therefore a very important mantra for the panchanga shuddhi as it is a mantra for the Sun god as well. Doing the Gayatri daily will help bring light back into a life that a difficult panchanga may have been obscuring.

Moksha Mantra and Maha Mrityujaya Mantra
Om Tryambhakam yajamahe
sugnadhim pushivardhan
Urvarukamiva bandhanan
mrityor moksheya mamratat Om

The meaning of this mantra is that we worship the three-eyed one (Shiva) who is fragrant and nourishes all beings. Just as a cucumber falls from its creeper and is detached from bondage, so Shiva will help us liberate the soul from death and find moksha (self-realisation) and amrita (the nectar of immortality).

This is also known as the moksha mantra and chanted by those who are seeking self- realisation and moksha. It is one of the best mantras for panchanga shuddhi as it bestows long life, peace, wealth, prosperity, satisfaction and immortality. It helps those who are ill, or who suffer from fears, depression and worry. This is one of the mantras constantly given by Parashara for remedial measures. It will not only help for panchanga shuddhi but is ideal for other difficult planets as well.

Hare Rama Hare Krishna
Hare Rama Hare Rama, Rama Rama Hare Hare
Hare Krishna Hare Krishna Krishna Krishna Hare Hare

The meaning of this mantra is that we chant the name of Rama and Krishna. It is a mantra for Vishnu and it works very well as a japa because you can repeat its sounds.

How to Plan the Mantras and Japa Practice
You should set aside time daily to do your mantra practice. If you are doing yoga or meditation, these can be added to them. You should sit in a lotus or half lotus pose facing east in the morning or north in the evening. The early morning or evening is the best time for this. Doing the gayatri and moksha mantra regularly is the best remedy for a difficult panchanga. You could add the Sun and Moon mantras to this as well.

Weekly, you should do a planned japa, using any of the mantras and repeating them at least 108 times. Make a commitment and stick to it. If you can commit to a daily japa, then do so. Otherwise weekly is good.

The main thing to remember is to do them with devotion with your mind involved in the practice. Focus on the clearing of your inner energy and slowly you will find that the blocks clear and the light becomes stronger. Do remember that it takes time. Do not expect instant results.

Daan – Donation: Giving your Time, Support and Money

Donation to the right causes is considered one of the most important remedial measures. You can donate your time and give support and money to worthy causes. Making the world a better place for others is an excellent way to cleanse your panchanga. If you cannot afford to give financially, give time. Supporting the poor and giving towards education and knowledge are two very worthy causes. You must give often. Giving on your birthday, the monthly tithi day and at important festivals is a good time, but donation must be done regularly and should become part of your life.

Path of Yoga – Mental, Physical and Spiritual Clearing

Following the eightfold path of yoga is a panchanga shuddhi in itself as it teaches all the tools required to cleanse and enlighten the soul. Some of the most important aspects of this path are speaking the truth, performing the right actions, doing meditation, mantras and japa, following the discipline of yoga asana, a proper diet, and a non-violent life dedicated to higher knowledge. This is a difficult path for most to follow but even to follow a part of it helps cleanse the panchanga.

Honouring the Sun and Moon Gods

Both the Sun and Moon are considered living gods, and honouring them daily would help to bring in light. Meditating at sunrise, doing the surya namaskar (salutation to the Sun), gayatri and Sun mantras, respecting and looking after your father, are some of the ways to honour the Sun. Meditating on the Moon at night, doing the moksha and the Moon mantras, feeding the poor, respecting and caring for your mother, are some of the ways for strengthening the Moon.

Sun and Moon Mantras

As the Sun and Moon are the important components of the panchanga, doing these mantras would be very beneficial. Do them on Sunday and Monday respectively. You can also make a japa out of them.

Surya (Sun) Mantra
Japakusuma Sankasham
Kashyapayem Mahadyutim
Tamorin Sarva Papaghnam
Pranotasmi Divakaram

Like the Kusum flower, son of Kashyapa, the great light
Destroyer of tamas and ignorance and all the sins
The lord of the day, Sun, I salute to you with every breath

Chandra (Moon) Mantra
Dadhi Shankha Tusharabham
Kshiridarnava sambhavan
Namami Shashinam Somam
Shambhomukuta Bhushanam

Like white curd, like white like snow, who emerged out of the ocean of milk
I chant the name of Shashi and Soma (Moon), who adorns the crown of Shiva

Honouring the Gurus and Brahmins

Gurus (teachers of higher knowledge) and brahmins (priests) should be honoured and supported regularly by giving them time and money to help with their educational work. You must honour the teacher, even if you think teachers are less than perfect, as they represent your pathway to higher knowledge. If you honour the teacher who is teaching you at present, you will attract better and better teachers. It is the gurus who show the way to the light.

Brahmins are priests. By supporting your spiritual organisation and its priest, you are helping bring light into your life. Usually brahmins are fed by gifts given to them at each yagya. You can plan to give an annual gift to them when you visit your spiritual organisation.

Feeding The Poor

This is one of the best remedies to do. You should feed the poor through donating food on your birthday, on wedding anniversaries or other special occasions. You can donate to a food bank or do anna danam at the local temple. Anna danam is donating of food but is usually connected to feeding the devotees at the temple. Most temples have a regular programme for this.

Seva and Karma Yoga – Looking After People and Voluntary Service

Giving service to others is a great way of doing inner cleansing. It can be done as voluntary work for a charitable organization or personally by looking after the elderly, the poor; giving time to make the world a better place for those who are needy. Seva means giving service to your parents, gurus or elderly people during their time of need. It should be done as a regular practice. Karma Yoga is voluntary work that makes life easier for all.

Following the Dharmic Path

Doing the right thing, following a path of dharma, is an excellent way of ensuring that you are bathed in light. Not only does it take care of the past by purifying the negativity, it also makes certain that your future is radiant.

9

FINDING YOUR TRUE LIGHT –
PANCHANGA ANALYSIS

While the natal chart represents a map of the heavens on the day of birth, panchanga reveals the five sources of light from that day. Both need the exact time and place of the nativity but which comes first – the rashi chart or the panchanga? While learning Jyotish, it is essential to study the rashi chart analysis first as I have done in *The Essentials of Vedic Astrology* and then to study the panchanga. Many elements of panchanga can only be understood once we have grasped the fundamentals of vedic astrology. It is essential to analyse them both simultaneously as one affects the other. It is like a flower and its perfume; both are intrinsic to each other. I am using two charts as examples: the international football star David Beckham and the singer Whitney Houston.

David Beckham is an internationally known football star who has played for Manchester United (1992 to 2003) and Real Madrid (2003 to 2007) football clubs, and was the captain of the English national football team from 15 Nov 2000 to 2 July 2006. He is married to Victoria Adams, 'Posh Spice' from The Spice Girls group, and they have three sons together. David joined the Los Angeles Galaxy team in the American soccer league in July 2007 for a five-year deal at $250 million dollars. He is the highest paid footballer in the world and as famous off the football field as he is on – known for his fashion sense, hair, tattoos and endorsement of many products and featuring regularly in advertisements. He is a tabloid darling and forever chased by the paparazzi.

Whitney Houston with her sensational voice and many consecutive number one singles and albums has also acted in films including *The Bodyguard* and has been a model and a film producer. She was one of the brightest shining stars of the 80s and 90s, when suddenly her whole world appeared to come apart. She married singer Bobby Brown and became addicted to drugs, her behaviour became erratic, and her career simply exploded into a downward spiral. Bobby Brown was often in prison and theirs was a turbulent and dysfunctional relationship. She became a shadow of her former self – gaunt, depressed and shabby. Finally, she divorced Bobby Brown in 2007 and is trying to get her old life together.

We have one person who has a supportive relationship and successful career and the other who suffered the classic decline of a troubled diva. What would their panchangas reveal? Whitney Houston has been living in a kind of darkness where the only news about her for many years has been negative, whereas David is the golden boy/man of sports and media who has successfully managed to navigate the tricky waters of success, celebrity and fame.

Step One: The Basics

David Beckham – Rashi Chart and Panchanga

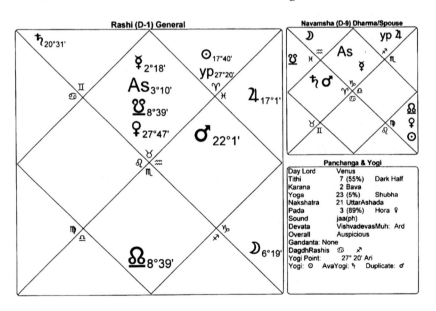

David Beckham – Natal Chart
Born at 06.17 hours BST on 2 May 1975, Leytonstone, England.

YP = Yogi point

David Beckham

The ascendant is 3°10 Taurus in Krittika nakshatra. The ascendant ruler Venus is in Taurus (27°47) in Mrigasira nakshatra. Venus is in its own sign, and in a kendra (cardinal) house it creates the Malavya yoga. Venus as the planet with the highest degree is also atmakaraka.

- Ketu at 8°39 and Mercury at 2°18 also rise in Taurus in Krittika nakshatra.

- Venus and Mercury as rulers of the 1st and 5th house create the Raja yoga. Ketu gives him an unusual personality.

- Sun is exalted at 17°40 Aries in the 12th house in Bharani nakshatra.

- The Moon is at 6°19 Capricorn in the 9th house in Uttara Ashadha nakshatra.

- Mars is at 22°01 Aquarius in the 10th house in Purva Bhadra nakshatra.

- Jupiter is at 17°01 Pisces in the 11th house in Revati nakshatra.

- Saturn is at 20°31 Gemini in the 2nd house in Punarvasu nakshatra.

- Rahu is in 8°39 Scorpio (Anuradha nakshatra) and Ketu is at 8°39 Taurus (Rohini nakshatra), both are debilitated and span the 7th and 1st house axis.

- Mars is in Aquarius ruled by Rahu and Rahu is in Scorpio ruled by Mars. This is Parivartana Yoga[1], which makes both planets very strong and improves their quality.

Navamsha

Venus and Saturn are debilitated while Mars is in Aries.

Dashas

Sun from birth to 23 Dec 1976
Moon from 23 Dec 1976
Mars from 23 December 1986

---

1.   Parivartana yoga is mutual exchange, when two planets make a connection by being placed in signs ruled by each other.

	David Beckham Panchanga				Sunrise 5.34		Sunset 20.22
1	Dina	Lord	Hora	Bhuta	Vela	Prakriti	Day Nakshatra
	Friday	Venus	Venus	Vayu	Rajas	Kapha-Vata	Ardra
2	Nakshatra	First Dasha	Nama	N Bhuta	Nakshatra Gandanta		
	U Ashadha	Sun	Jaa	Vayu	None		
3	Tithi	Paksha	Type	T Bhuta	Tithi Gandanta		Dagdha Rasi
	Saptami	Krishna	Bhadra	Prithvi	none		Cancer, Sag
4	Karana	Lord					
	Balava	Moon					
5	Yoga	Yogi point	Yogi	Duplicate Yogi	Avayogi		
	Shubha	27°21 Aries	Sun	Mars	Saturn		

David Beckham – Panchanga in detail

Rahu from 23 Dec 1993
Jupiter from 24 Dec 2011 to 24 Dec 2027

This is a strong chart with many positive aspects. At present David is in a Rahu dasha which is debilitated and placed in the 7th house, making a positive parivartana with Mars in the 10th house.

Whitney Houston – Rasi Chart and Panchanga

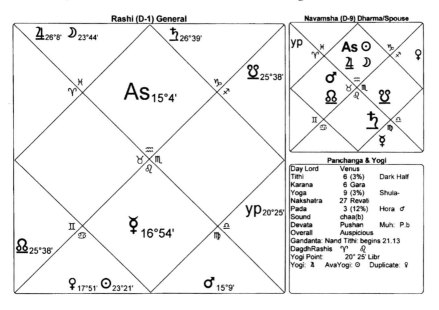

Whitney Houston – Natal Chart
Born at 20.55 EDT on 9 August 1963, Newark, NJ, USA.
YP = Yogi Point

(The bhuta changes at 20:53 from vayu to aakash, therefore she could have been born slightly earlier as the vayu bhuta can be more self-destructive. We should look at this chart as being born on the cusp of two bhutas).

The ascendant is 15°04 Capricorn in Shatabhishak nakshatra. It is vargottama. If we move her time back by two minutes to achieve the vayu bhuta, it will still remain vargottama and the degrees would change to 14°14 Aquarius.

The ascendant ruler Saturn is retrograde at 26°39 Capricorn in Dhanishta nakshatra. Saturn is in the 12th house in his own sign and is also the planet with the highest degree and atmakaraka. Whitney's lagna is also her atmakaraka, just like David's. But there are two fundamental differences. Her lagna ruler is retrograde and in the 12th house – both factors increasing the unsteadiness in her personality and life.

- The Sun is at 23°21 Cancer in the 6th house in Ashlesha nakshatra.

- The Moon is placed at 23°44 Pisces in the 2nd house in Revati nakshatra. It is in Gajakesari yoga[2] with Jupiter.

- Mars is at 15°09 Virgo in the 8th house.

- Mercury is at 16°54 Leo in the 7th house.

- Jupiter retrograde is at 26°08 Pisces in the 2nd house. This forms Hamsa yoga[3] from the Moon.

- Venus is placed at 17°51 Cancer in the 6th house. It is combust.

- Rahu/Ketu are in Gemini/Sagittarius, and span the 5th and 11th house axis.

Navamsha
The lagna is vargotamma – the same sign rises in the lagna and the navamsha.

The atmakaraka and lagna ruler Saturn goes to Leo and the 7th house.

Dashas
Mercury from birth to 1 Aug 1971
Ketu from 1 Aug 1971
Venus from 1 Aug 1978
Sun from 1 Aug 1998
Moon from 1 Aug 2004
Mars from 1 Aug 2014

---

2. Gajakesari yoga is formed by Jupiter and Moon in the same house or in kendras from each other, located in kendras from lagna or Moon.
3. Hamsa yoga is formed by Jupiter in its own house or exalted from the lagna or the Moon. It is one of the Mahapurusha yogas.

Whitney Houston Panchanga					Sunrise 5.59		Sunset 20.06
1	Dina	Lord	Hora	Bhuta	Vela	Prakriti	Day Nakshatra
	Monday	Moon	Mars	Aakash	Sattva	Kapha -Vata	Ardra
2	Nakshatra	First Dasha	Nama	N Bhuta	Nakshatra Gandanta		
	Revati	Mercury	Chaa	Aakash	None		
3	Tithi	Paksha	Type	T Bhuta	Tithi Gandanta		Dagdha Rashi
	Shashti	Krishna	Nanda	Agni- fire	yes		Aries, Leo
4	Karana	Lord					
	Gara	Jupiter					
5	Yoga	Yogi point	Yogi	Duplicate Yogi	Avayogi		
	Shoola	20°25 Libra	Jupiter	Venus	Sun		

Whitney Houston – Panchanga in detail

Step Two: The Strength of the Sun and Moon

The Sun and the Moon are the vital components of the panchanga and their natal positions support the panchanga and the natal chart. Points to consider are the natural quality of the Sun and Moon and whether they are strong in their own house, whether or not they are exalted, or in a friend's house with aspects or conjunction with the benefics (Jupiter, Venus, Mercury) – the house position does not matter so much. A difficult house position would just show the inability to understand the Sun and the Moon, but their inherent quality is strong. Their weakness by debilitation, enemy signs, combustion, conjunctions with malefic planets, or difficult aspects of Saturn, Mars and Rahu and Ketu will not be improved by being in a good house. Saturn's aspect is the toughest one to have.

David Beckham – his Sun is exalted. It is in Obhayachari yoga, supported by benefic Mercury and Jupiter on either side and there is no malefic aspect at all. This is a strong Sun and its strength is not lessened by its placement in the 12th house. His Moon is in Capricorn (enemy sign), and is waning but it is still quite visible on saptami in the night sky. It has the 9th house aspect of Ketu, which can make his mind troubled at times. The Moon is not as strong as the Sun for Beckham, but both are free from Saturn's aspects. The overall quality of the two luminaries is better than average and therefore will support the chart and panchanga.

Whitney Houston – her Sun is in Cancer (friend's sign) in the 6th house. It combusts Venus, therefore it takes on some of the positive qualities of Venus. The Sun is quite strong but this is spoilt by an exact aspect from Saturn by opposition. The Moon is in Gajakesari yoga in the 2nd house in the neutral sign of Pisces but its aspects from Saturn and Mars harm the yoga detract from its strength. The Moon is in krishna shashti tithi, which is still strong in the night sky. Saturn is blocking both the Sun and Moon. The luminaries have their positive points and negative ones – at times they obscure the picture and at others they give support.

Step Three: The Dina

David Beckham			Dina	Sunrise 5.34		Sunset 20.06
Dina	**Lord**	**Hora**	**Bhuta**	**Vela**	**Prakriti**	**Day Nakshatra**
Friday	Venus	Venus	Vayu	Rajas	Kapha-Vata	Ardra
Whitney Houston			Dina	Sunrise 5.59		Sunset 20.06
Dina	**Lord**	**Hora**	**Bhuta**	**Vela**	**Prakriti**	**Day Nakshatra**
Monday	Moon	Mars	Aakash	Sattva	Kapha-Vata	Ardra

The dina is always analyzed first as it gives the primary energy to the personality. The lord of the day shows the principle energy and the lord of the hora shows how this energy will be used. Then we will study other aspects of the dina: prakriti from the lord of the dina, the rising bhuta, gunas from the vela, and the day nakshatra.

The Dina Lord
The dina lord's strength gives the person confidence to do what they want to do and supplies the force to complete their spiritual tasks. The dina lord's weakness can make the soul feel troubled about its purpose, insecure and unable to use its energy properly. This is the first judgement to make, as the strength of the dina lord is vital for the rest of the chart. A lack of strength can create all sorts of problems in the rashi chart as the soul struggles to express itself properly, so the dina lord should be fortified. Wearing gems would not be the right remedial measure in this case; puja, donation, mantras and following the higher path of the dina lord would be better.

David Beckham – the dina is Friday and the lord is Venus, who is his lagna lord, atmakaraka and placed in the lagna creating Malavya yoga and Raja yoga. This is a very strong dina lord. It gives him the ability to achieve whatever he wants. Ketu's presence with the dina lord can create problems at times, as David may not recognise his qualities, but usually Ketu acts like the planet it is placed with, so further adding strength here by duplicating all Venus' powers. Venus gives a love of good things, creativity and style. David is known as much for his sporting abilities as for his fashion and media presence. Venus is the karaka for the wife and Victoria Beckham is a powerful support in his life – treating his wife with respect would be a daily remedial measure.

Whitney Houston – her dina is Monday and the lord is the Moon. The Moon is the 6th lord and the 6th lord always creates problems and obstacles where he is placed. Accordingly she may feel she is forever facing challenges in her life. However, the Moon is placed in the 2nd house and in Gajakesari yoga with Jupiter. The 2nd house rules the voice and she has a beautiful voice and this has been her great gift provided she did not think of the gift as a hindrance. The aspects of Saturn and Mars on her Moon can make her doubt her talents and good inheritance. Honouring and supporting her mother would be a good remedy for Whitney to strengthen her dina lord.

The Role of Sun and Mars
The Sun and Mars play a very important role in the overall energy of the chart. As the dina represents the agni bhuta, the quality of Mars and the Sun in the natal chart should be analyzed as this will show the all-embracing energy the individual has brought into life.

David Beckham – his Sun is exalted in Aries and Mars is in the 10th house in dik bala[4], and although the Sun in this house and can show a misuse of his energy, it is exalted and very strong. Both the Sun and Mars give him plenty of power and energy to do what he wants. It gives physical strength, ambition and varied desires; ability that is essential for such a high level sportsman.

Whitney Houston – her Sun is in Cancer in the 6th and Mars is in Virgo in the 8th. Both are less than ideal. The Sun in Cancer is not always good for energy as the water quality can put out the fire of the Sun and bring a lack of confidence, poor self-esteem, and low energy levels of acceptance of life as it is. There is no drive to fight the demons or be ambitious. When Whitney's problems started, she may well have passively accepted what was happening. Mars in Virgo in the 8th shows a misuse of

---

4.   Dik bala means directional strength – Planets are at their strongest in certain houses.

its energy. Mars is in its enemy house and the earth element of Virgo could have smothered the fire of Mars and thus any energy Whitney had. When this happens Mars usually struggles to express its power even more and takes on an aggressive quality that can create frustration and anger.

Dina Lord versus Sun and Mars

The dina lord gives added energy and if it is strong it can override the conditions of the Sun and Mars. If Mars and the Sun are weak in the chart but the dina lord is strong, it can use their energy in the right way, making the most of it, whereas if the dina lord is weak, it can misuse even the good energy.

David Beckham – all three components, Venus, the Sun, and Mars are strong and therefore he has lot of energy to accomplish what he wants. His ambitions are great but he has the nerve to achieve them. His desires can be too grandiose and this can make him feel dissatisfied unless he learns to control them. As the dina lord is the atmakaraka and the lagna ruler, the energy flows very easily.

Whitney Houston – she has problems with both Mars and the Sun. Her dina lord is in a good yoga but unless she counts her blessings, the rulership of the dina lord of the 6th house makes her misuse her energy. The Moon and the Sun are both aspected by Saturn giving her spikes of energy and disturbing its smooth flow.

Dina Lord in the Rashi Chart

If the dina lord is the atmakaraka then the atma's purpose will be most served as the soul feels in tune with its higher purpose and gains extra ordinary strength to fulfil its mission. If the dina lord is the lagna lord, the soul will give more credence to this incarnation rather than the bigger picture of the atmakaraka. If the dina lord is the Moon lord, then the emotions and intuition dominate. Similarly you can study the other lordship of the dina lord to understand what it is that the soul is reflecting in the natal chart.

David Beckham – his dina lord is atmakaraka, lagna ruler and in many yogas. It is very strong. His has a mission to accomplish in this life and enough power to do so.

Whitney Houston – her dina lord is also the 6th lord but is placed in the 2nd house and with Jupiter in Gajakesari yoga. She has used her energy for singing and she may appreciate this great inheritance. She can be emotional and highly-strung.

The Dina Lord and its Connection to the Lagna

David Beckham – the dina lord and lagna lord are the same and in the lagna a very good combination for achievement.

Whitney Houston – the lagna lord is placed in the 11th house from the dina lord – a good combination. The problem lies with the lagna lord being in the 12th house, she may easily get distracted from life. The Moon and Saturn do not have a good relationship, so they may not always work in harmony with each other.

Hora Lord

If the hora is atmakaraka, it will influence the soul to follow the soul path but may not be able to change its direction. If on the other hand the hora is the lagna lord, the lagna will follow the atma and this creates harmony with the purpose of the incarnation. An inimical hora lord can try to take the soul in the wrong direction while a friendly one will help. If the hora and dina lord belong to conflicting bhuta, there can be problems. If dina is the Sun and hora is Venus, their respective bhuta are fire and water. The fire and ambition of the Sun will be dampened by the actions of Venus.

David Beckham – dina and hora lord is Venus. There is complete harmony between both of them.

Whitney Houston – dina is the Moon and hora is Mars, bringing conflicting elements of fire and water. The soft emotional energy of the Moon can get disrupted, heated up or even completely used up by Mars, which is also placed in the difficult 8th house. Hot and cold passions, too much or too little energy, and living with anger can be the fallout from this.

The Rising Bhuta

This is the special quality within you which can influence your prakriti and nature. It will also show whether you express the male or female qualities. The bhuta can easily get out of control and become a dosha. The rising bhuta shows a soul focusing more on the spiritual path while the falling one will show an inclination towards materialism.

David Beckham – the rising bhuta is arohi vayu which rises from 6.04am to 6.28am. The time would have to change quite a lot if he was to have a different rising bhuta – vayu is female by nature and David does have feminine qualities including his voice, which is very thin; he also has a great interest in clothes, fashion and the body beautiful. His swiftness of feet and mastery of football can also be considered a vayu quality. This is an arohi vayu, therefore he is more active and aggressive. Vayu has a connection with Kubera, the god of wealth, and David has shown great talent at making money.

Whitney Houston – her rising bhuta is arohi aakash, which rises from 20.53 to 21.21 hours. If her birth time was a few minutes earlier, she could easily be avarohi vayu bhuta (20.29 to 20.53). Aakash has male energy and often the tabloids have alluded to her being gay. Vayu can be much more self-destructive than aakash and the many years of her negative life style can be attributed to the avarohi vayu. Arohi would make it active while avarohi would entangle her further in her weaknesses. I feel she is born on the cusp between these two elements, which can give her either quality and can also increase her confusion and sense of insecurity.

Prakriti and dosha

Prakriti is nature and this is found from the dina lord and the rising bhuta. If they are weak or negatively placed in the rashi chart the prakriti can become troubled and therefore become a dosha or weakness.

David Beckham – his prakriti from the bhuta is vata and from the dina is kapha. Saturn rules vayu and Venus expresses kapha. Saturn is placed in the 2nd house in Gemini, a neutral position for Saturn by house and in its friend's sign, so it will not become a weakness easily. Also Venus is strong so will have the positive qualities of vata and kapha. Speed, agility and mental brightness will come from vata. Calmness under crisis, wisdom and flexibility will come from kapha.

Whitney Houston – her prakriti from the bhuta is on the cusp of vayu and aakash (vata and kapha) and from her dina lord the Moon also kapha and vata. This shows a person with many turbulent emotions. It is easy for her to live by her emotions but not be able to control them when they spiral downward. The Moon and Jupiter both have their strengths and weaknesses and she could quickly regain her strength through yoga and mediation.

Rising Guna

David Beckham – is born in rajovela, therefore has the seeking quality of rajas guna. This gives him success, fame and an active mind. He is ambitious and seeks success.

Whitney Houston – is born in sattovela and has the softness of sattva. Inside, her mind is pure and she can be spiritual and lustrous. This is the quality she must seek. The lustrous quality of the young Whitney was perhaps reflecting sattva. Her roots lay in gospel music and her fame at an early age may have obscured the spiritual qualities that still underly her personality.

Dina Nakshatra

This is analysed to see further modifications as the nakshatra always shows the mental make up. See if any planet is placed in the dina nakshatra and how the nakshatra ruler is placed in the natal chart. The deity of the dina nakshatra protects your energy. If your dina nakshatra is Ashwini, the position of Ketu in the natal chart will give you extra information. Also Ashwini Kumaras are the cosmic physicians and this gives interest in healing and medicine. You can further study all aspects of Ashwini and the other nakshatras from *The Essentials of Vedic Astrology*.

David Beckham – the dina nakshatra is Ardra. Rudra, the god of destruction is the presiding deity. David has never taken the destructive path of Rudra but rather the more constructive one. As his dina, lagna and atmakaraka are so strong, this gives him the ability to be empowered and use his qualities in the best possible way. Shiva is a deity revered by millions and so is David. The only aspects of his life that he changes regularly are his style of dressing, and hairstyle; there is a new Beckham nearly every year. I am not sure how much internal change has taken place. He has also lived in different places – London, Manchester, Madrid and now Los Angeles. He is still young, so he may move around a lot more yet. At each stage of life dissatisfaction must have led him to start expanding toward differing horizons. The principle of Ardra can be said to destroy what we create, so David needs to be careful, but as his lagna lord is so strong, he may never go down that path.

Rahu is the ruler of Ardra and David is in Rahu dasha. Lots of his changes have taken place in this dasha. Rahu is also in the 7th house showing support from relationships – this is the area of life he must be most careful not to destroy. He has no planet in Ardra.

Whitney Houston – the dina nakshatra is Purva Bhadra. There is no planet placed in this nakshatra. Purva Bhadra can feel ugly because on a subtle level these people are seeing the issues of their karma clearly and it is not very appealing. They can make themselves suffer with image problems in the material world unless they take the step forward, overcome their fears, and find the ideas they are generating can make the world a lot better. I feel that this is where the problem lies for Whitney – the public have seen her as an exalted diva with the world at her feet but within her own mind she could never reconcile this image. The public and personal life did not match and this could have led to all her problems. Purva Bhadra is lonely yet can sustain life for others. It is also a very spiritual nakshatra and the key may lie in Whitney re-exploring her spiritual path. The ruler of Purva Bhadra is Jupiter and this is a strong planet for her. She should consider moving towards the goal of wisdom and taking a slightly different path from that of a pop singer/diva.

Step Four: The Nakshatra

David Beckham				
Nakshatra	First	Nama Dasha	Bhuta Nakshatra	Nakshatra Gandanta
U Ashadha	Sun	Jaa	Vayu	None

Whitney Houston				
Nakshatra	First	Nama Dasha	Bhuta Nakshatra	Nakshatra Gandanta
Revati	Mercury	Chaa	Aakash	None

The quality of the mind

The nakshatra is a very important element of the panchanga as it studies the mind. Although other aspects of panchanga and the natal chart will influence this quality, it is the nakshatras that decide how the mind is, what blocks it has inherited and how it deals with life in general. The Moon and its nakshatra decide the dashas and when we are going to have the most difficult transit of all – sade sati – the 7½-year transit of the Moon by Saturn.

David Beckham – Uttara Ashadha people are creative and talented and can have god-given gifts like David has for football. Often it is seen with Uttara Ashadha that these people believe in conspicuous consumption. They may have big parties, huge homes or anything bigger than they can afford, but their temperament is quite ascetic – they do not always appear to enjoy the material trappings and live a frugal life despite all the money. David has always shown an inclination for grand gestures and a life lived entirely in the media, but this is a soul looking in the wrong place. As he grows older, the other side of his personality – the more ascetic and philosophical – will come out. His spiritual journey will be more personal, not one he wants to talk to the world about.

He may worry that he may not have enough to care for his family and this can lead to him working harder and harder. The Moon struggles initially to embrace the austerity of Uttara Ashadha, so will go through mental stresses until it truly finds its own place. David may be a solitary man despite the entire world that surrounds him.

The Sun rules Uttara Ashadha and is exalted in his natal chart, so will give him the best qualities of that nakshatra – the mind benefits.

Whitney Houston – Revati nourishes others and I see this quality in Whitney, but she may not be making a wise choice in those whom she cares for. It is easy for the Pisces Moon and Revati to become a victim, as they do not always have an easy ability to live in the material world. She must have faced disappointments with the people she met and this is hard for the idealistic Revati to handle. Really the soul demands spirituality and the mind will remain disturbed if it is living totally in the materialistic world. Spirituality makes the Revati Moon most happy and this is what Whitney should explore.

The First Dasha and the Karmic Pattern of the Life
The dasha gives a life path but one has flexibility within this; we can follow the path to the best or worst of our abilities. As the dashas are connected to the Moon, they show the changing needs of the mind. Knowing the dasha patterns helps us to keep in tune with the development of the mind and the altering landscape of our life.

David Beckham Dasha Patterns

Dasha	From	To
Sun	2 May 1975	23 Dec 1976
Moon	23 Dec 1976	23 Dec 1986
Mars	23 Dec 1986	23 Dec 1993
Rahu	23 Dec 1993	24 Dec 2011
Jupiter	24 Dec 2011	24 Dec 2027
Saturn	24 Dec 2027	24 Dec 2046

David began his life with a Sun dasha. The Sun is exalted in his chart and placed in the 12th house. The dasha lasted for a short time, but it left a good impression on his psyche. There is a past life connection to the exalted Sun and in his mind he may feel that he was a great personality before and so can aspire to it again. With the Sun being in the 12th house though, he may not always be comfortable with his power.

He had the Moon dasha till the age of 11. This would have expressed the loneliness of Uttara Ashadha. He would have been a loner as a child and his personality may not have come out totally. He describes himself as shy and introverted in his biography.

The Mars and Rahu dashas are interconnected as they are in parivartana yoga. Mars in the 10th secured him an early contract with Manchester United (the biggest football club in England) in July 1991 during Mars Ketu. Ketu is in the lagna with and acting like Venus – his atmakaraka, lagna and dina lord. Rahu established him as a star. Rahu moves from 7th to 10th due to the parivartana and so although it may trouble his mind, it is no longer debilitated but in the best house. The Rahu dasha has brought him international fame: his true personality and genius only came out in the Rahu Jupiter when he hit the headlines in August 1996. Rahu Saturn introduced him to his wife, Victoria and brought international fame when he was part of the Manchester United Team that won the treble of the League, Championship and European Cups in 1999. Marriage to Victoria also took place in July 1994. Saturn rules the nakshatra of Rahu, which is placed in the 7th house.

In 2011 when he moves to a Jupiter dasha, he may change his career and life path.

Whitney Houston Dasha Patterns

Dasha	From	To
Mercury	9 Aug 1963	1 Aug 1971
Ketu	1 Aug 1971	1 Aug 1978
Venus	1 Aug 1978	1 Aug 1998
Sun	1 Aug 1998	1 Aug 2004
Moon	1 Aug 2004	1 Aug 2014
Mars	1 Aug 2014	1 Aug 2021
Rahu	1 Aug 2021	1 Aug 2038

Whitney Houston was born in a Mercury dasha. Mercury is in the 7th house and she may have identified with relationships and marriage in her subconscious from an early age.

She belongs to a family of singers; Ketu in the 11th house would have given her the great connection with gospel singing and the church.

During Ketu dasha Rahu bhukti, Whitney sang for the first time in front of the congregation at New Hope Baptist Church in Newark. But Ketu usually rejects what it aspires to and at the end of the dasha she moved from gospel to singing, acting and dancing.

Venus dasha saw an amazing rise for Whitney Houston but its end also contributed to her equally spectacular decline. In 1983 during Venus

Venus she was signed to Arista Records and in March 1985 her first album was released during Venus Mars. Her marriage to Bobby Brown was in 1993 during Venus Saturn dasha.

It was the start of the Sun dasha in August 1998 when the decline in her career and her life became obvious. The Sun is the avayogi planet; it is combust Venus and it is a negative planet from both lagna and the Moon. Knowing the dasha could have minimized the problem, but Whitney's panchanga is difficult, suggesting she may not be seeing her life in its true light. The Sun dasha lasted from 1998 to 2004, when she had to face all sorts of issues, including arrest for drugs, a break with her father, problems with her husband and many episodes of drug rehabilitation.

She began her Moon dasha in 2004, and it was during Moon Rahu that she finally divorced her husband in 2007 and got custody of her child. She begins her Mars dasha in 2014.

Her dasha pattern has not been so kind to her after the great Venus dasha – Sun is avayogi, Moon rules the 6th house, Mars is placed in the 8th – for a long time she may have to struggle against the odds. These struggles may be easier to cope with if she follows a spiritual life, whereas trying to remain purely in the material world may aggravate them more. The Sun was her most difficult dasha and she has already faced that, so life can get better.

The Role of Saturn
Saturn is the lord of vayu and Rahu also influences it on a subtle level. Whereas other bhutas need to be strong, vayu needs to be kept quiet as it can be destructive if strong. The winds of the mind should be like gentle breezes not violent storms. Saturn or Rahu can directly influence the Moon by conjunction, aspects or by their transits. Saturn has many difficult transits directly connected to the Moon – sade sati, ashtama shani (including the 64th navamsha and the 22nd drekkana transits) and kantaka shani. These are detailed in *The Essentials of Vedic Astrology*. Rahu will bring his impact through eclipses as well. Saturn aspects the 3rd, 7th and 10th houses and Rahu the 5th, 7th and 9th houses from themselves, so if they aspect the Moon, they will create disturbances.

Essentially both Saturn and Rahu need to be controlled, pacified and propitiated. Doing maha mrityunjaya mantra and japa regularly would keep them calm. Fasting for Saturn and praying to Shiva would be other good remedies. These could help everyone regardless of the quality of their Saturn and Rahu.

David Beckham – does not have Saturn or Rahu conjunct the Moon but his Moon is placed in Capricorn, Saturn's Sign, and he could therefore experience the qualities of Saturn. His Saturn is strong and in Gemini. When Saturn is in a friend's house, it is calm; it is more troubled in negative houses. David does have a practical and responsible mind and may worry whether he can take responsibility and fulfill his duties properly. Saturn does not aspect the Moon either.

Saturn can trouble the Moon by its transits. From 15 July 2007 to 10 Sept 2009, Saturn is in Leo, which is the 8th house from the Moon. This is ashtama shani, not a good transit for health and relationships but can be good for career. It appears that David is experiencing a great time having landed a multi-million dollar deal in American soccer, but the transit suggests that this deal may not be satisfying for him in the end. It could lead to problems. One of the many influences of this transit has changed his life style and made him move home from the UK to USA. The sages considered moving to a far away land a very negative action, but the pinnacle of this ashtama is when Saturn transits over the 64th navamsha.[5] The 64th navamsha falls from 3°20 to 6°40 Leo for David and Saturn will transit these degrees from 12 August 2007 to 7 September 2007 – fortunately just once for him. He will need to be careful during this time as ashtama shani is negative for health, so may bring injury problems. David's next sade sati begins on 26 October 2017.

There are two important eclipses that David should watch out for. The lunar eclipse on 7 Feb 2008 at 5°54 Leo, which is close to his 64th navamsha position, could bring immediate problems regarding health, reputation or relationships. Then there is a solar eclipse on 22 July 2009 at 5°27 Cancer, which is opposite his Moon. Solar eclipses have a longer time influence and may show him making yet another change in his life. This eclipse follows the Rahu transit over his Moon on 21st July 2009.

---

5.   64th navamsha falls in the 8th house from the moon. 64 navamshas are counted from the birth Moon, treating the navamsha it is placed in as one. The 64 navamsha is a difficult point in the chart and when planets transit, it can cause crisis.

Although its influence appears far away, he can plan for it by making sure he reconciles his life regularly, not leaving behind too many loose ends.

Whitney Houston – Her Moon is in Pisces with Jupiter. While this is a positive Gajakesari yoga and Jupiter helps the mind, both have aspects of Saturn and Mars. Her vayu element is disturbed and she would be perpetually searching for peace of mind. Lack of clarity does lead to making wrong decisions and she needs to work at calming the mind and being detached all the time, not just during negative transits.

Whitney experienced her first sade sati from 5 March 1993 to June 2000. Its greatest intensity was in June 1997, when she was ending her Venus dasha. Her state of mind would have then been the most troubled. Usually during the start of sade sati one makes a decision which can create huge problems for the future. In 1993, right at the start of this period, she married Bobby Brown and a lot of people felt this was the biggest mistake of her life. It is difficult to say whether he brought all her problems, but according to vedic tradition we choose our own karma so Bobby Brown may have been the manifestation of what she needed to face and deal with. We cannot put all the blame on him.

Rahu was in Aquarius during the Moon Rahu dasha when she finally divorced him. The public felt she should have done it long before but the troubled mind and the high vayu in her chart makes it tough for her to make decisions. She should try to be in a low stress job or have a strong spiritual regime. There are no exact eclipses for Whitney's Moon and in 2006/2007 they were in the Leo/Aquarius axis when she finally gained courage to cut off her ties with Bobby Brown.

Nama Nakshatra
The name given at birth should help calm the mind if it is rightly chosen according to its nakshatras and pada. If has not been chosen according to vedic rules, one should check which nakshatra and house the name falls in.

David Beckham – the birth name should have been Jaa from the third pada of Uttara Ashadha. The alphabetic sound of David – 'Da' – falls in the third pada of Ashlesha. This is in the third house of confidence, communication and media and a good place for the name nakshatra. It is an upachaya house, which improves constantly and gives courage and confidence.

Transits to the position where the name nakshatra rests in the chart can either give prominence to the individual or create problems. The third pada of Ashlesha falls between 23°20 and 26°40 Cancer. Saturn transited these degrees from 27 August to 24 September 2006 at which time he had been written off by the world's media and generally considered a has-been star. When Saturn transited these degrees again from 27 Feb to 24 June 2007, David's name was never out of the news – mostly due to his deal with LA Galaxy. Saturn is his Raja yoga karaka but it is also the avayogi planet, so both the qualities of Saturn were evident in this transit through complimentary and adverse press coverage.

Whitney Houston – the birth alphabet should start with Cha from the 3rd pada of Revati. But the name 'Whitney' would come from Vee from the third pada of Rohini. In Sanskrit there is no difference between V and W. Rohini falls from 20° to 23°20 Taurus, which is Whitney's 4th house. This is a very positive place and therefore this name is very good for her. I was not expecting anything else, as she is so famous, but the transit of Saturn or other planets over this point can either bring fame or infamy. The 2002 conjunction of Rahu, Saturn and Mars over these degrees on 6 June 2006 was accompanied by a huge story of Whitney's father, John, suing her.

The Bhuta of the Nakshatra
David Beckham – his nakshatra bhuta is vayu, which connects to the heart chakra. He is a double vayu person, and his mind is as fast as his feet. Vayu gives him a quick thinking mind and practicality, but it can also make him a worrier. Anahata chakra teaches one to be detached and to love all. His mind can never be still and he would have to develop mediation and mantra practices to keep it under check. David is supposed to be greatly disciplined and maybe he already practises control of mind in his routine.

Whitney Houston – her nakshatra bhuta is aakash, which connects to the vishuddhi chakra. Aakash shows her as a high-minded person. There is an ethereal quality about her that brought her so many fans, but the ability to purify which vishuddhi chakra has, is lessened by the aspects of Saturn and Mars on both the Moon, which is essentially vayu by nature, and Jupiter who rules the aakash bhuta and vishuddhi chakra.

Nadi Nakshatras

These are special nakshatras derived from your birth nakshatra – some good and others difficult. Avoid people with nakshatras that are difficult and embrace those who are friendly. Transits to these nakshatras can give different experiences according to their nature.

David Beckham: Nadi Nakshatras

Janma nakshatra – the 1st nakshatra – is Uttara Ashadha, the same as at his birth. If his parents, brothers, sisters, or children were born with the same nakshatra, he would need to do remedial measures, but as I do not have their birth data it is not possible to check. Victoria Beckham[6] has Dhanishta or Shatabhishak nakshatra.

Karma nakshatra – the 10th nakshatra from janma is Krittika. Transits to this nakshatra and people with this nakshatra would be helpful for him professionally and help him accomplish the right karma. David has his ascendant, Ketu and Mercury, in Krittika nakshatra and this gives him great support to forward his life agenda. During the dasha and sub-dashas of these planets too he will make great progress.

Sanghatika nakshatra – the 16th nakshatra from janma is Ashlesha, which creates wrong associations, and people with this nakshatra are to be avoided. Also when malefic planets cross this nakshatra David should be wary of people he associates with. Saturn was in Ashlesha for most of 2006 till 15 July 2007. This is the time he signed the new contract with Los Angeles Galaxy and moved to the USA. He should have been careful of new associates at that time. Maybe the contract and association with LA Galaxy is not as glittering as it looks.

---

6.   Victoria Beckham – born on 17 April 1974, Hertfordshire, UK. Time not known. Her year of birth is often given wrongly as 1975.

Samudaya nakshatra – the 18th nakshatra from janma and an auspicious one. This is Purva Phalguni for David. Ketu transited in late 2006 and early 2007 in this nakshatra and Saturn will from August 2008. Both would bring more luck to him. Those with Purva Phalguni Moon or ascendant and Sun would be great for him.

Vinasha nakshatra – the 23rd from janma – is the most negative nakshatra. This is Vishakha nakshatra for David. From 9 January to 4 May and 9 September to 12 November 2006 Jupiter transited through this nakshatra and was not a very good time for him. During this period Saturn was also transiting in Ashlesha, his sanghatika nakshatra and the press universally castigated his performance in the World Cup 2006 and he lost his position on the England team as well as his captaincy.

Manasa nakshatra – the 25th from janma. Jyeshta is the 25th nakshatra and shows his mind. It is interesting that this falls in the 7th house of his chart, confirming that he does wants marriage and relationships. Jyeshta deals with power, secret knowledge and the individual's struggle to master their destiny. David is known for his fine disciplined nature. He may already have developed the ability to control any weakness he may possess, physical or mental. This comes from a Jyeshta mind. He will also have great desires and a highly sensuous nature.

Whitney Houston: Nadi Nakshatras

Janma nakshatra – the 1st nakshatra – is the same as birth and is Revati. Again it is difficult to know if her family has any of the same nakshatras and the remedies that were required.

Karma nakshatra – The 10th nakshatra from janma is Ashlesha. Transits through Ashlesha or people with an Ashlesha Moon can be a great help to Whitney. Saturn had been transiting Ashlesha for most of 2006 till 15 July 2007, and whereas for David Beckham this sanghatika transit was not good, for Whitney it would have been a great time for career and making positive changes. It was during this transit that she finally had enough courage to divorce Bobby Brown.

Sanghatika nakshatra – the 16th nakshatra from janma is Swati. Whitney has suffered from the bad company that this nakshatra suggests, but without data of the people involved in her life it is difficult to make any correct analysis. Jupiter transited there in 2006 but there is no major transit there now for some time although the faster moving planets like Sun, Mars, Venus and Mercury will do so regularly. The Moon will be in this nakshatra on a monthly basis and she should be careful of the people she meets at those times plus people with Moon or planets in Swati.

Vinasha nakshatra – the 23rd from janma is Shravana. Bobby Brown,[7] her husband, has his Sun in Shravana nakshatra. This relationship has been extremely rough on Whitney and she lost her career and reputation during her time with him. Having the Sun in a Vinasha nakshatra meant that Bobby could bring out the worst level of Whitney's ability to self-destruct. This is an extreme case as Whitney's own Sun is very negative being avayogi, dagdha lord and the 7th lord. When someone appeared with this Sun, the latent qualities were awakened.

Manasa nakshatra – the 25th from janma is Shatabhishak and her lagna is in this nakshatra. Shatabhishak can be the hundred healers or the hundred demons; maybe she has dealt with both sides of this coin. Shatabhishak churns up the mind in pursuit of the nectar of self-realisation. In this search for eternal happiness the first experience is toxic and poisonous, and can be in the form of drug or alcohol abuse, bitterness, jealousy, obsessive relationships etc. Once the soul goes beyond that, it starts seeing the beauty and the light of being Shatabhishak. Considering Whitney's mind is already distressed, Shatabhishak can make it more neurotic if she is not careful. Also as her ascendant falls in this nakshatra, she is already dealing with Shatabhishak and this gives a double dose so it is up to her which aspect of this nakshatra she embraces. It is important to remember that quieting the mind is not easy without having a plan for it. Yoga and chanting would be the best remedies for her.

---

7.   Bobby Brown, born 5.21 am, at 5 Feb 1969, Boston, MA, USA.

Gandanta or Difficult Nakshatras

Neither David or Whitney were born in the difficult nakshatras.

Nakshatra for Prayers

David should give Capricorn Uttara Ashadha as his nakshatra when visiting a temple and Whitney should give Revati.

Step Five: Tithi

David Beckham	Krishna Saptami		
Type	T Bhuta	Tithi Gandanta	Dagdha Rashi
Bhadra	Prithvi	none	Cancer, Sag

David Beckham – Tithi is krishna saptami. The Sun rules it, and David with his exalted Sun can personify all the qualities of this tithi including the desire to succeed and to be someone. His fans pray to him to show his best side and shine his radiance on them, and he is thus following the cult of Surya. Although at the moment the public are dazzled by him, his is an illusionary light and one day his fame could disappear. His desires can be enormous, as he wants to achieve, have the best and the biggest, but he is also a self-disciplined person and when he finds dissatisfaction from material goals he may become more spiritually inclined. Arrogance can be a problem and also the possibility of many relationships. David's fixed lagna Taurus does keep him in one relationship but he needs to beware. Krishna paksha makes him more introverted despite all the glitz, not always willing to voice his deeper thoughts. Bhadra tithis have the practical prithvi bhuta, supportive towards relationships, so he is always ready to be there for his partner.

Whitney Houston Krishna Shasti			
Type	T Bhuta	Tithi Gandanta	Dagdha Rashi
Nanda	Agni	yes	Aries, Leo

Whitney Houston – Tithi is krishna shashti. Mars rules it and it is placed in the 8th house in the enemy sign of Virgo. It is also one of the nanda tithis, and that is tough on relationships. Whitney was born at the beginning of the nanda tithi which is Gandanta; there are spiritual lessons to be learnt along with extreme insecurity regarding relationships. The fiery shashti is unable to support the apas, the overall bhuta of the tithi. It heats up the waters and creates great passions but can also dry them up. These people allow their emotions to rule them and Whitney Houston must suffer terribly from emotional insecurities. She wants support from relationships but is attracted to those who are unable to offer them. Her public persona may also overpower the relationship with her husband and others who are trying to compete with her fame.

The deity is Kartikeya, who can conquer all. Whitney won over millions of fans with her singing and acting but Kartikeya also rules the ego and Whitney may have suffered from this. Her immense fame may have made her forget that fame is not just her making, it is maya – illusion. Shashti have to learn to restrain their ego and surrender to the divine forces and usually they have to learn from their experiences and cannot take advice easily.

The Role of Venus
Venus is the ruler of apas bhuta and the karaka of relationships. A good Venus can improve the negativity of nanda tithis.

David Beckham – has a strong Venus and this brings in a steady relationship and supportive wife despite any other attractions.

Whitney Houston – has a strong Venus is placed in the difficult 6th house, is combust and aspected by Saturn. Venus is hot and passionate yet is hidden behind the light of the Sun. In women's charts I find this creates an inability to understand their femininity, they crave for relationship but do not know how to express their own female desires properly. Saturn's aspect is forever creating distances from loved ones and troubling the emotions. Despite living in the same celebrity world as David Beckham, her relationships are much more difficult and complex.

Dagdha Rashi
Burnt rashis and their rulers create problems in the chart. Read the exceptions in the Tithi chapter as they must be used as an added on

feature – don't base your entire analysis of the chart on this. Dagdha rasis can spoil otherwise good indications but they cannot take all the goodness away.

David Beckham – Cancer and Sagittarius are his dagdha rasi. Cancer rules the 3rd house and Sagittarius rules the 8th house, and there are no planets in these houses. Usually when the 8th house is combust, it takes away the negative qualities of the 8th house so it is an improvement. Jupiter, the dagdha lord, is placed in the 11th house – all planets are well placed there – so this improves Jupiter and makes it less malefic. This has given him immense wealth but he may not enjoy it or feel totally happy despite the enormous amounts he earns.

The Moon as a dagdha ruler of Cancer is placed in the 9th house and this can cause problems with the father or a guru. David does not have any obvious problems with his father, but he had a very open disagreement with Sir Alex Ferguson, the manager of Manchester United that led him to leave the club. Managers in football are often like father figures to their young players.

Whitney Houston – Aries and Leo are dagdha rashis and Mars and the Sun are the lords of dagdha. Her 7th house is Leo, Mercury is placed in it, the ruler Sun combusts Venus; it is also an avayogi. Whitney has all the signatures of complex and troubled relationships. There are too many indications adding to the already difficult story. The Sun dasha would have been the most traumatic, as it bought together all the negative qualities of the Sun. Bobby Brown became the person through whom she experienced it.

Aries rules her 3rd house and this would affect her confidence and relationship with siblings.

Tithi Gandanta
David Beckham was not born on tithi Gandanta whereas Whitney was. She was born at the start of nanda tithi, making her feel more insecure. As this tithi primarily deals with emotional happiness and relations, it would accentuate them even more.

Tithi Pravesh

There are twelve tithis similar to the birth tithi that repeat monthly. One of these is the maha tithi or the great tithi and is celebrated as the birthday. The chart of the time when the tithi is exactly as in the birth chart is known as tithi pravesh and is analyzed as an annual chart. The monthly tithi chart can be studied too for finer analysis.

David Beckham – his tithi return is monthly, on krishna saptami. Annually when the Sun is in Aries and it is krishna saptami, it will be David's maha tithi and the tithi pravesh chart should be studied to understand what the year ahead has in store for him.

In 2007, the maha tithi pravesh was on 9 May 2007 at 7:31am, London. In 2007 David changed both his job and his country so what does the chart indicate? It has a Gemini ascendant with Mercury, the ruler, in Taurus in the 12th house of loss and foreign countries. The 12th lord Venus is in the ascendant. The Moon is in the 8th house, again indicating sudden transformation. The exalted Sun in the 11th house will show lots of money being made through his own efforts (3rd house ruler). I tend to blend the tithi pravesh chart with the solar return chart to help me get an overview of what is happening. The tithi was showing clearly a smooth changeover to a far-off place, but David will still hanker

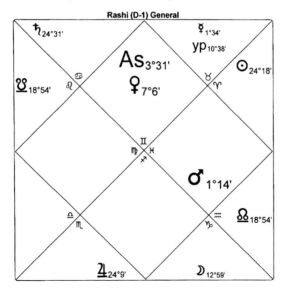

David Beckham – Maha Tithi Pravesh was on 9 May 2007

after his life in UK. As it is a tithi pravesh, be careful to read it for a year only. One great advantage David Beckham has is that annually on his tithi as well as solar returns, his Sun is exalted. Unless the Sun is afflicted in the annual chart he always gets added strength from this. More detail can be studied in the chart; I have just focused on the salient features.

Whitney Houston – her tithi is krishna shashti and this will be her mini-birthday each month, while the maha birthday will be annually when the Sun is in Cancer. The predicament for Whitney is that she annually revisits her tithi Gandanta, which re-enforces her insecurities, unlike David Beckham's annual chart which re-enforces his strengths. Whitney finally divorced Bobby Brown and got custody of her child on 8 April 2007, which is apparent in her 2006 tithi pravesh. The ascendant is Scorpio, (her natal 10th house), and the ruler Mars is well placed in the 10th house. This gave her strength to do what she had been avoiding for so long. The Moon in the 5th house shows the mind focused on her daughter. The Moon is vargotamma further giving mental strength. The divorce is indicated here as the 7th house ruler and significator of marriage, Venus, is conjunct Mercury, the 8th house ruler (8th house usually deals with divorce or transformation), and Jupiter, the significator of the husband, is in the 12th house of loss.

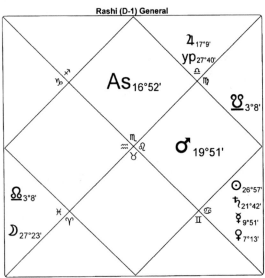

Rashi (D-1) General

Whitney Houston – Maha Tithi Pravesh was 13 August 2006

Step Six: Karana

Karana supports the tithi but even a good karana cannot give full support if the tithi is Gandanta. Karana rulers show the profession and all professions are not listed in the notes, so readers can add more as they go along. A person may also reflect the quality of their karana ruler through their profession. It is important to study the position of the karana ruler in the chart and its nakshatra dispositor.

David Beckham

Karana	Lord
Balava	Moon

David Beckham's karana balava shows a strong mind. David has clear thinking in guiding his career and life. Balava are popular people and this is essential for those who are public favourites. They are strong minded, powerful, brave, pleasure loving, sensuous, poetic and artistic, and can be involved in many relationships. The Moon is placed in the 9th house in Uttara Ashadha nakshatra showing a solitary person who believes in following his dharma, self-discipline and responsibility. David Beckham may not take the usual lunar route of multiple partners and is instead ready to commit to one person, but this is through discipline not natural inclination. Usually Balava people are always on the move, and this would express itself in his career as a footballer where he needs to be fast and also his jet-set lifestyle. The Moon's nakshatra ruler is the exalted Sun in Aries, indicating an adventurous, sporty person who has great leadership qualities. All of which David has shown aplenty! The 9th house is the 5th from the 5th and as the 5th house is generally regarded as the house for sport, the 9th house will reflect those qualities too. The Moon in Uttara Ashadha and Capricorn gives David Beckham the ability to be disciplined and focused on his task.

Whitney Houston

Karana	Lord
Gara	Jupiter

Whitney Houston's karana is gara, which means destroying poison and Jupiter rules it. These people can be judicious, liberal and physically well proportioned. They can control their negative traits and have special skills in dealing with poisons: actual and of the mind. Whitney has a beautiful body, which has suffered through self-abuse. Her well-known drug problems show that she is unable to detoxify herself even though her karana says she has the ability to do so. Although Jupiter is in Pisces, it is not a good planet for Aquarius lagna, as it may not be naturally motivated to do the right thing for her. It also suffers from aspects of Saturn and Mars – both distorting it and not allowing it to function properly, and it is placed with the Moon, the 6th house ruler. They are in Gajakesari yoga and the negative aspects cause it work less efficiently. But Jupiter's placement in the 2nd gives a clear indication of her profession as it deals with inheritance, voice and face – important factors in her success. She sings, she is beautiful and she inherited the talent from her mother and family. Also Jupiter is placed in a Mercury ruled nakshatra, Revati. Mercury is the actor, writer and entertainer.

The Role of Mercury

Mercury rules prithvi bhuta and its strength or weakness in the chart would define how practical an individual is and how they can guide their career. It is important to remember that Mercury is extremely changeable and its rulership of earth and the career indicates the changeable and insecure nature of life itself.

David Beckham – has Mercury rising in dik bala[8] in the 1st house. It is in Taurus, a friend's house and in Krittika nakshatra, which is ruled by the exalted Sun. This is a strong Mercury and therefore gives a sound underpinning to his career. Ketu's influence on Mercury brings an unconventional flavour.

Whitney Houston – has Mercury in Leo which is a dagdha rashi and Mars and the Sun hem it in. There was never satisfaction for Whitney regarding her career and her prithvi bhuta is not stable. Her Mercury does become exalted in the navamsha – but it goes into the 8th house, which will show major fluctuations. While dagdha rashi and the hemming in of Mercury does influence her life negatively, it still gave her a strong

---

8.   Dik Bala is directional strength. Mercury has it in the 1st house.

career. Also Mercury lacks directional strength as it is opposite to the 1st house where it gets maximum strength. The practical side of Whitney does not work very well and she is open to dominating influences from other people.

Step Seven: Nitya Yoga

David Beckham	Nitya Yoga Shubha	
Yogi point Yogi	**Duplicate Yogi**	**Avayogi**
27°21Aries Sun	Mars	Saturn
Whitney Houston	Nitya yoga Shoola	
Yogi point Yogi	**Duplicate Yogi**	**Avayogi**
20°25 Libra Jupiter	Venus	Sun

Nitya yoga gives the ultimate balance to the panchanga. If there is a good yoga, it will help all the other elements to perform well. If the yoga is negative, you must perform regular remedial measures to provide the support and sustenance the soul needs.

David Beckham – his Nitya yoga is Shubha. This means 'auspicious' and it brings him lots of blessings. He will feel a sense of well being and be able to understand his problems, and the light of the panchanga works well for him. It does not mean that life will always be smooth sailing, but when trouble arrives he will be able to deal with the issues it brings successfully.

Whitney Houston – her Nitya yoga is Shoola, a tough yoga to be born under. Shoola means pain, and Whitney can feel the piercing energy of this yoga. It gives her an aggressive attitude despite her being a good person overall. She needs to be careful of the abusive side of this nakshatra which not only means she can mistreat and abuse others but that she can get involved in abusive relationships in return. Shoola does not offer protection and security to her and she can remain in the dark about her weakness for a long time.

The Role of Jupiter

Jupiter as the ruler of aakash bhuta is the planet that provides protection and its position in the natal chart is essential. A strong Jupiter can improve the yoga while a weak Jupiter can make a good yoga less potent.

David Beckham – has Jupiter in Pisces in the 11th house of profit. This is a strong Jupiter. All planets in the 11th house are well placed. Saturn aspects Jupiter with its 10th aspect and Rahu aspects it with the 5th, so it does make it less secure, but Jupiter along with Mercury is part of Obhayachari yoga[9] on the Sun. Jupiter goes into Sagittarius in the navamsha, giving it deeper strength.

Whitney Houston – has Jupiter in Pisces but it is retrograde and also has aspects from Mars and Saturn. Retrograde planets can easily go off track or become unstable. Retrograde Jupiter is very strong, yet he does not provide protection and stability to the person who has it. In her heyday people may have mistaken her strong Jupiter for a secure one. The aspects don't help either. Jupiter is not able to help the pain of shoola.

Yogi Point, Yogi and Duplicate Yogi

David Beckham – has the Sun and Mars as yogi and duplicate yogi. Both are sporty and powerful and help David in his quest for success. The yogi point is 27°21 Aries. The Sun is exalted though placed in the 12th house promising success abroad. Also I have noticed that many very successful people have Sun in the 12th house. As the 12th is the next house the Sun moves into after it rises, the 12th house is a strong and visible Sun. Successful people tend to have visible power and fame whereas they may not feel the same about their fame and power internally. How we see them and how they view themselves may be totally different, so a 12th house Sun should not be taken as negative for success. Mars is in the 10th house representing both sports and ambition. The yogi point in Aries means that when the yogi and the duplicate yogi planets cross this point, the Sun is exalted and Mars is in its own house, further reinforcing the luck while the avayogi Saturn is debilitated by transit.

---

9.   Obhayachari Yoga happens when two benefics hem in the Sun.

The avayogi transit will happen only once in 29 years whereas the Sun crosses the yogi point annually and Mars every two years.

Whitney Houston – yogi is Jupiter and duplicate yogi is Venus. I have written quite a lot about Jupiter and its strength in this analysis but the yogi planet in the 2nd house of voice and face gave Whitney great beauty and a marvellous singing voice. The malefic aspects indicate problems in expressing this. Those who have seen pictures of Whitney recently can see the decline from the stunning beauty she once was. Her duplicate yogi is combusted by the avayogi planet, therefore not always able to give its best.

The good news is that Venus crosses this point annually, the 9th house ruler in its own house by transit and crossing the yogi point. The last time when Saturn, her lagna lord, crossed this point in 1984 (three times: 2 Jan 1984, 4 April 1984, 28 Sept 1998) she was recording her first album. Not only was the lagna lord exalted, it crossed the yogi point as well – a very special time for her. She must have felt on top of the world. Saturn will cross this point just once on 8 November 2013. She has to expect something good at that time too, maybe in a different way. Her lagna lord is always exalted when it crosses the yogi point.

Avayogi
David Beckham – avayogi is Saturn, which is also his rajayogakaraka, the 9th and 10th house ruler and the best planet for Taurus rising. How do you reconcile these two opposites? Firstly the rajayogakaraka will take precedence but usually during the dashas, sub-dashas or transits of Saturn there may be some problems due to its avayogi nature. Good and bad coming together. During Rahu Saturn dasha, David Beckham as the captain of Manchester United won the English Premiership, FA Cup and UEFA Championships Treble. He got married to Victoria as well. But he had a much-publicized row with his manager Sir Alex Ferguson during this time about Victoria Beckham's influence and his lack of attention to his training and club. Sir Alex and David's relationship became damaged irreparably. The fame and celebrity that Saturn brought as rajayogakaraka created problems between the club and David's time away from it. That would also be the work of Saturn as an avayogi.

Whitney Houston – avayogi is the Sun. The Sun rules her 7th house and is also the ruler of the Leo dagdha rashi. The Sun dasha from 1 Aug 1998 to 1 August 2004 tarnished her career, reputation and life almost beyond repair. As the Sun rules the 7th house, most of her problems came from her relationship with Bobby Brown. The Sun is the karaka of the father and there was bad blood between Whitney and her father when his company sued her in 2000. When he died in Feb 2003, Whitney did not attend his funeral. Usually the avayogi is not so devastating but in Whitney's chart the Sun takes on many negative roles and she experienced its dasha after a great Venus dasha, so it was more negative than usual. When you see multiple factors coming together it creates a major crisis in life.

Step Eight: Chakras

The chakras expressed through the panchanga reveal the subtle energy within the chart. As the soul settles into the subtle body, materialism may totally obscure its true needs. Most people don't search for their chakras but may have already opened some of them unknowingly giving themselves the appropriate skills and qualities. If a person goes on a spiritual path these chakras bring access to the higher self and allow one's eyes to open to a deeper and more subtle knowledge. For David Beckham and Whitney Houston we are looking at their spiritual balance through the chakras.

David Beckham

Muladhara is connected to prithvi mahabhuta and Mercury. This chakra indicates the balance in life through which the soul can develop upward. If the world and earthly affairs are not in balance the upward movement of the soul cannot take place. Mercury is strong in David's chart and therefore he has a solid platform for his spiritual life to move upwards – he is ready for it.

Swadhisthana is connected to the apas mahabhuta and Venus. This chakra shows the proper expression of emotional balance and sexual desires. Venus is very strong in his chart and indicates he has the mastery of this chakra. He will be sensitive and emotional but not allow feelings to go out of control easily. The Moon also has an influence in this bhuta and as his Moon is more ascetic this will keep a check on Venus's more sensuous side.

Manipura is connected to agni mahabhuta and Mars. This chakra shows the fire of ambition, of desires and needs. On a spiritual level it also shows the spiritual fires that can burn away all the negativity created by past karmas. Mars deals with the more material desires whereas the Sun is spiritual. Mars is very strong in the 10th house and can give him grand ambitions, which he must try to control. But the fire of Mars has also given him sporting skills. This can also make him egoistic and stop his spiritual growth. The Sun is exalted in the 12th house – this is a strong indication for a spiritual fire burning within and something through which he can develop. Manipura chakra is working very well.

Anahata is connected to vayu mahabhuta and Saturn. This chakra deals with love and detachment. To be truly on the path of the higher self one has to learn to detach from this world and love people unconditionally. These are the teachings of Saturn. As Saturn is his avayogi planet, it may not always be able to do this. Vayu is quite high in David's chart but he can master it as his other chakras are working well.

Vishuddhi is connected to aakash mahabhuta and Jupiter. This deals with the soul's ability to process the negativity in life and make it positive. David Beckham was born under Shubha yoga, which means despite some weakness to Jupiter, he is able to deal with the negativity and purify it. This is a great blessing for him.

Most of the chakras are working pretty well and if David ever wanted to progress to a more spiritual life, he will be able to connect to his chakras and make them work well. He may need to work with his anahata chakra and learn to detach. The Rahu dasha he is in at present will keep him focussed on more material things, but Jupiter may make the difference. As life on the material realm is working well for him, he may not make the effort to work on his chakras.

Whitney Houston
Muladhara is connected to prithvi mahabhuta and Mercury. It deals with the balance in material life. Mercury is placed in the dagdha rashi

in the 7th and hemmed in by malefics. She is seeking her balance from relationships and they can let her down. Mercury is not stable at all and she needs to work to make this chakra work.

Swadhisthana is connected to the apas mahabhuta and Venus. Venus brings creativity, sensitivity and sensuality. Her Venus is strong but combust. During her Venus dasha, this chakra was working well but in the Sun dasha it would have burnt out its power. She would need to be very conscious of her Venusian qualities and preserve them. The Moon is the secondary ruler of this chakra and is reasonably well placed, but the aspects to it do not help. It can give too much sensuality that keeps her tied to her emotions.

Manipura is connected to agni mahabhuta and Mars, showing the fire of ambition and desires. Mars is in the 8th in the enemy sign and is also a dagdha lord, which shows a dysfunctional Mars. It can give ego, anger and desires that she would not know how to control. Material issues can obscure her more spiritual ones. The Sun is avayogi and will not therefore naturally guide her towards burning past karma, it will be more interested in creating new karma especially during its dasha from 1998 to 2004.

Anahata is connected to vayu mahabhuta and Saturn. Saturn is strong but retrograde and in the 12th. The vayu element is very high here and it is therefore difficult for her to be detached from the world. As I have explained earlier, you need vayu to be calm. She can worry, be anxious and the mind is not always at peace but Saturn is in its own sign and she can bring it under control if she tries.

Vishuddhi is connected to aakash mahabhuta and Jupiter. This allows her to detoxify from the world but her life has shown it is not easy for her. Although Jupiter is in its own house, in hamsa and Gajakesari yogas from the Moon, it is the Shoola Nitya yoga that does not allow this chakra to function properly.

The picture of Whitney Houston's chakra appears very dire but all is not lost. Usually the negative elements are at their worst when one is searching purely in the material life. In Bhagawad Geeta, Shri Krishna tells Arjuna that when vishad (sorrow) happens, it is then the soul thinks of its higher self. Those who have a difficult chart need to focus more on the spiritual and less on the material, then it would give them rich rewards.

Step Nine: Remedial Measures

David Beckham – all panchanga elements work together and the Nitya yoga brings very good protection to him, therefore he has the ability to see his chart and life in a good light. I would recommend him to continue with his charity work and bring yoga into his life. His life to the outsider seems to be one of great consumption and he should try to curb his desires. He has also used his celebrity to do many good and charitable deeds and this would further enhance his qualities. He could do remedial work for Saturn, his avayogi, by working with the poor and needy.

Whitney Houston – has a tough panchanga. This creates the inability to recognise her true strengths and weakness. My strategy for her would be firstly to focus on her insecurities. Mercury as the ruler of muladhara chakra is a good planet for her and it is moving towards exaltation. Its placement in the dagdha rashi and in the 7th house does create problems. The deity for Mercury is Vishnu and getting a puja done in the temple and chanting the Hare Rama Hare Krishna mantra or Om Namah Narayana would be the best starting point for her. The Indians believe that Christ is also an incarnation of Vishnu and she could do hymns and visit the church to create the base of security around here as well.

She needs to practice inner yagya, through the path of yoga, chanting, japa and donation. I would suggest to her chanting the maha mrityunjaya mantra daily to give her protection. She could also chant it when she feels afraid or worried about anything.

Her Sun is the most difficult planet; it brought problems with her husband and her father. It also blocks her manipura chakra. She must do remedial measures for the Sun, including reconciling mentally with her father as he is no longer alive for her to physically resolve. She must try to do shraddha for her father annually – giving a donation in his name, feeding his favourite foods to friends and the poor, chanting the gayatri mantra daily to energize the Sun to show its most benefic side to her.

She could also consider going back to her roots in gospel music and follow a more spiritual path. Doing charitable work and feeding the poor would be a very good way to further add to her subtle protective layers. She could use her celebrity to make life better for the poor and needy.

Remedial measures done with a full heart take time, but slowly they would change the way she thinks and help her lead a more positive and constructive life. Although she is not directly trying to make herself feel insecure, the remedies would create a buffer and enable her to build up a subtle protection.

Whitney could follow her own way if she does not want to follow the vedic remedies, but she should consider doing the vedic chants as they have a special subtle vibration – she would benefit from them. Doing a japa of the chants and maybe doing them 108 times or even 1008 at a stretch would also help bring peace of mind.

She should follow a new path and not necessarily try to recreate the past. This would bring her the greatest happiness.

BIBLIOGRAPHY

Further Reading

The Essentials of Vedic Astrology by Komilla Sutton, published by The Wessex Astrologer, Bournemouth.

The Lunar Nodes by Komilla Sutton, published by The Wessex Astrologer, Bournemouth.

Myths and Symbols of Vedic Astrology by Bepin Bihari, Lotus Press, Twin Lakes, WI.

Esoteric Astrology by Bepin and Madhuri Bihari, published by Sagar Publications, New Delhi.

New Techniques of Prediction by H S Seshadari Iyer, published by Janapriya Prakashana, Bangalore.

Nakshatras by Dennis M Harness PH.D. Published by Lotus Press, Wisconsin.

Path of Light (*Parts One and Two*), by James Kelleher, published by Ahimsa Press, San Francisco, CA.

Reference Texts

Brihat Parashar Hora Shastra translated by Girish Chand Sharma, Sagar Publications, New Delhi , India.

The Brihat Jatakam of Varaha Mihira translated by Swami Vijnanananda, published by Oriental Books Reprint Corporation, New Delhi.

Phaldeepika by Mantreshwar, translated by G S Kapoor, Ranjan Publications, New Delhi.

Jataka Bharnam by Pandit Dhudiraj, translated by Girish Chand Sharma, Sagar Publication, New Delhi.

Hora Ratnam by Balabhadra, translated by R. Santhanam, published by R Santhanam Associates, New Delhi.

Jataka Parijata by Vaidyanatha Dikshitha, translated by V Subramanya Shastri, published by Ranjan Publications, New Delhi.

Saravali by Kalyan Varma translated by V. Subramanya Shastri, published by Ranjan Publications, New Delhi.

Varaha Purana, translated by Venkitasubramonia Iyer, published by Motilal Banarasi Das, Delhi.

Muhurta by B V Raman, published by UBSPD, New Delhi.

Muhurta Chinatamani by Daivagya Acharya Shri Ram, translated by Girish Chand Sharma, Sagar Publications, New Delhi.

Spiritual Texts

The Principal Upanishads by Dr. S Radhakrishnan, published by Indus, New Delhi.

The Bhagavad Gita by Swami Sivananda, published by the Divine Life Society, Rishikesh.

Raja Yoga by Swami Vivekananda, published by Advaita Ashrama, Calcutta.

Bhakti Yoga by Swami Vivekananda, published by Advaita Ashrama, Calcutta.

Atma Bodha by Sri Adi Shankaracharya with commentary by Swami Chinmayananda, published by Central Chinmaya Trust, Mumbai.

Tattva Bodhah by Sri Adi Shankaracharya with commentary by Swami Tejomayananda, published by Central Chinmaya Trust, Mumbai.

Tattva Shuddhi by Swami Satyasangananda, published by Yoga Publications Trust, Munger.

The Sivananda Companion to Yoga published by Simon and Schuster, New York, NY.

Puja compiled and published by The Sivananda Yoga Vedanta Center, Montreal, Quebec.

Practice of Nature Cure by Swami Sivananda, published by The Divine Life Society, Rishikesh.

Chakras by Harish Johari, published by Destiny Books, Rochester, VT.

Light on the Yoga Sutras of Patanjali by B K S Iyengar, published by Harper Collins, New Delhi.

Light on Yoga by B K S Iyengar, published by Harper Collins, New Delhi.

Ayurveda, The Science of Self Healing by Dr. Vasant Lad, published by Motilal Banarasidas, New Delhi.

Vedic Astrology Software

1. Shri Jyoti Star website – www.Vedicsoftware.com
2. Parashara's Light website www.Parashara.com
3. Goravani Jyotish Studio website www.Goravani.com

Lightning Source UK Ltd.
Milton Keynes UK
UKOW04f2009070314

227770UK00001B/3/P